C000130709

# Into Touch

*Dedicated to my extraordinary children without whom there would be no point*

*Luke, Emily and Rebecca*
*With all my love*

# Into Touch

## Rugby Internationals killed during the First World War

Nigel McCrery

Pen & Sword
**MILITARY**

First published in Great Britain in 2014
and republished in this format in 2022 by
Pen & Sword Military
An imprint of
Pen & Sword Books Ltd
Yorkshire – Philadelphia

Copyright © Nigel McCrery 2014, 2022

ISBN 978 1 39902 010 7

The right of Nigel McCrery to be identified as Author of this work has been
asserted by him in accordance with the Copyright, Designs and Patents Act 1988.

A CIP catalogue record for this book is available from the British Library.

All rights reserved. No part of this book may be reproduced or transmitted in any
form or by any means, electronic or mechanical including photocopying, recording
or by any information storage and retrieval system, without permission from the
Publisher  in writing.

Typeset in 10pt Dante by Mac Style
Printed and bound in the UK by CPI Group (UK) Ltd, Croydon, CR0 4YY.

Pen & Sword Books Limited incorporates the imprints of Atlas, Archaeology,
Aviation, Discovery, Family History, Fiction, History, Maritime, Military, Military
Classics, Politics, Select, Transport, True Crime, Air World, Frontline Publishing,
Leo Cooper, Remember When, Seaforth Publishing, The Praetorian Press,
Wharncliffe Local History, Wharncliffe Transport, Wharncliffe True Crime, White
Owl and After the Battle.

For a complete list of Pen & Sword titles please contact

PEN & SWORD BOOKS LIMITED
47 Church Street, Barnsley, South Yorkshire, S70 2AS, England
E-mail: enquiries@pen-and-sword.co.uk
Website: www.pen-and-sword.co.uk
or
PEN AND SWORD BOOKS
1950 Lawrence Rd, Havertown, PA 19083, USA
E-mail: Uspen-and-sword@casematepublishers.com
Website: www.penandswordbooks.com

# Contents

# Contents

got the axe for a very brave action. It appears that he was one of five to go at midday and attempt to locate a machine gun and Turkish trenches. The sergeant got a rough time and was finally shot. Harold, after a while, found the corner too hot and taking the sergeant's body he made it back under heavy fire to the trenches. When he was preparing to get into the trench himself a bullet passed through his body low down.

He died from wounds on 10 May 1915 aboard ship after evacuation from Gallipoli. A funeral service was conducted by the chaplain from HMS *London* and Harold was buried at sea.

His club mate Clarrie Wallach, who also fought at Anzac Cove, wrote a letter home which was published in the sporting paper *The Referee*. He described hearing of George's death from William Tasker, another rugby contemporary who saw Gallipoli action and later died on the Western Front; 'Twit Tasker told me how Harold George died the death of deaths – a hero's – never beaten till the whistle went.' He is commemorated on the Lone Pine Memorial, Turkey (Panel 37).

His brother, 2520 Corporal Roy Wesley George, 45th Battalion, was killed in action at Dernacourt, France, on 5 April 1918. Their next of kin was given as their mother, Mrs E. George, Kemmis Street, Randwick, NSW.

## International Caps

25 June 1910. Australia (0) vs New Zealand (0) 6. Sydney Cricket Ground.

27 June 1910. Australia (3) 11 vs New Zealand (0) 0. Sydney Cricket Ground.

2 July 1910. Australia (5) 13 vs New Zealand (6) 28. Sydney Cricket Ground.

16 November 1912. USA (0) 8 vs Australia (5) 12. California Field, Berkeley.

6 September 1913. New Zealand (11) 30 vs Australia (5) 5. Athletic Park, Wellington.

20 September 1913. New Zealand (5) 5 vs Australia (5) 16. Lancaster Park, Christchurch.

18 July 1914. Australia (0) 0 vs New Zealand (0) 5. Sydney Sports Ground.

15 August 1914. Australia (0) 7 vs New Zealand (3) 22. Sydney Sports Ground.

**Captain Bryan Desmond Hughes MC**
**Royal Dublin Fusiliers**
**Died 6 August 1918**
**Aged 30**
**Flanker**
**Two Caps**

*'Still an Australian through and through'*

Bryan Desmond Hughes was born in Sydney in 1887, the son of Mr and Mrs John Hughes MLC. Educated at Saint Ignatius' College, a Roman Catholic Church School, Riverview, in Sydney, New South Wales, he played as a prop/hooker for North Sydney, NSW, and was considered an outstanding goal kicker; he converted two goals in Australia's 1913 victory over New Zealand.

On leaving school Hughes went to work for Birt and Co. Ltd, before joining John Bridge and Co. Ltd, as a clerk, both operating out of Sydney. After gaining some commercial experience he travelled to England to work for his uncle, Sir Thomas Hughes MLC, to study law. At the outbreak of the war he was commissioned into the 8th Battalion Royal Dublin Fusiliers (the same battalion as his brother Lieutenant Gilbert N. Hughes who was later engaged on Allenby's staff in Palestine). He went to France on 20 December 1915 and was quickly involved in some of the heaviest fighting of the war. Promoted to captain he went on to be awarded the Military Cross for bravery, the citation for which read:

> For conspicuous gallantry and devotion to duty. Though severely wounded, he organised the battalion bombers and led them against the enemy, who had penetrated a portion of the front line. It was largely owing to his personal example and good leadership that the enemy were driven out.

His MC was gazetted on 24 June 1916.

Seriously wounded again in 1917, he had only recently returned to the front when he was killed in action on 6 August 1918. He is buried in Borre British Cemetery, Nord, France (Grave II. G2).

## International Caps
13 September 1913. New Zealand (9) 25 vs Australia (8) 13. Carisbrook, Dunedin.
20 September 1913. New Zealand (5) 5 vs Australia (5) 16. Lancaster Park, Christchurch. 398

4

**448 Private Herbert (or Hubert) A. Jones**
**30th Battalion AIF**
**Died 4 November 1916**
**Aged 27**
**Centre**
**Three Caps**

'*Whatever Comes He Would Face*'

Herbert Webber Jones was born in 1888 to William Morris Jones and Mary Jones of little Young Street (now Roger Street), Carrington. He was one of six children, three girls and three boys. On leaving school he joined his brothers working as a coal trimmer on the Carrington docks. Jones played his rugby for Carrington (as well as several other local clubs). He played no fewer than twenty-one matches for New South Wales between 1911 and 1914 and toured the United States with the twenty-three-man Australian team in 1912 (although he did not play an international match). He toured New Zealand as a centre three-quarter in 1913, playing in three tests and scoring three tries.

Herbert Jones enlisted in the AIF on 26 July 1915 at the age of 26 years and 11 months. He was posted to the 30th Battalion of the newly formed 5th Division and embarked on the troopship *Beltana* on 9 November 1915. Herbert Jones was killed in action by shellfire on 4 November 1916, being the only member of the battalion killed on that day.

He is buried in the AIF Burial Ground, Grass Lane, Flers (Plot IX, row B, grave 4). As he was not married, his mother Mary was granted a pension of one pound per fortnight. It has been said that his last surviving sister Nell Beesley (Roger Street Carrington) donated Herbert's Australian and New South Wales touring caps to the Newcastle Regional Museum during the mid-1980s. However, having contacted the museum, they tell me they have no record of this.

## International Caps

6 September 1913. New Zealand (11) 30 vs Australia (5) 5. Athletic Ground, Wellington.

13 September 1913. New Zealand (9) 25 vs Australia (8) 13. Carisbrook, Dunedin.

20 September 1913. New Zealand (5) 5 vs Australia (5) 16. Lancaster Park, Christchurch.

For many years Herbert Jones has been confused with 6616 Herbert Jones, 20th Battalion AIF, who was killed in action on 9 July 1918 and is buried in Crucifix Corner Cemetery, Villers-Bretonneux, Somme, France (V E. I).

**321 Sergeant Edward Rennix Larkin**
**C Company 1st Battalion, AIF**
**KIA 25 April 1915**
**Aged 34**
**Hooker**
**One Cap**

*'In time of peace they readily asserted the rights of citizenship.*
*In time of war they fiercely protected them.'*

Edward Rennix Larkin was born on 21 September 1880 at North Lambton, New South Wales, the third child of William Joseph Larkin, a quarryman and miner, and his wife Mary Ann, née Rennix. Edward eventually moved with his family to Camperdown in Sydney and was educated by the Marist Brothers at Saint Benedict's School, Chippendale, Sydney. During his final two years at school he was boarded at St Joseph's College, Hunters Hill where, in 1896, he was selected to play for the college first XV.

On leaving school he first became a journalist working on the *Year Book of Australia*. Then in 1903 he joined the Metropolitan Police Force as a constable, being promoted to first-constable in 1905. At the time he joined he was described as five feet ten and a half inches (179cm), weighing thirteen stone (83kg), with blue eyes, brown hair and a fresh complexion. On 24 July 1903 he married his long-time girlfriend May Josephine Yates at St Joseph's Catholic Church, Newton, and they went on to have two sons.

As well as being a fine rugby player he maintained an active involvement in cricket and swimming. He continued his rugby union career, playing for the Endeavour Rugby Club at Newtown in Sydney and captaining the side in 1903. That year he played as a forward for the State against New Zealand and Queensland and was then selected to play for Australia in the first test at Sydney on 15 August 1903; on this occasion Larkin played hooker. The Australians were soundly beaten 22-3. He was not to represent Australia again.

A good and eloquent speaker, an ability he honed as a member of the St Joseph's (Newtown) Debating Society, he began to take an interest in politics and to have parliamentary aspirations. In June 1909 he left the police force and became the first full-time secretary of the New South Wales Rugby Football League. He was an excellent organizer and strongly promoted rugby league, as was clearly demonstrated when a crowd of 42,000 filled the Agricultural Oval in June 1910 to watch the Australia v Great Britain test. During his administration he also convinced the Catholic education hierarchy, and the Marist Brothers, to adopt rugby league as their winter sporting game. In 1911 he became a justice of the peace before standing as an Australian Labour Party candidate on 13 December 1913, winning the seat of Willoughby taking 51.61 per cent of the votes. While in parliament he became a vocal supporter for the building of a bridge across Sydney Harbour.

On 17 August 1914, only ten days after war had been declared, Larkin enlisted, joining C Company in the 1st Battalion, Australian Imperial Force, not as an officer which, given his position, would have been almost automatic in England, but as a private soldier. His talents quickly became apparent and he was soon promoted to sergeant. The 1st Battalion left Australia in October 1914, arriving in Egypt on 2 December. Larkin's battalion landed at Anzac Cove on 25 April 1915, one of the most infamous dates in Australian military history and one of its finest. Larkin was shot and killed by machine-gun fire while attempting to secure a hill known as Baby 700. When the stretcher-bearers came to evacuate him, although badly wounded and dying, he waved them on saying, 'There's plenty worse than me out there'.

He died a short while later. His brother Martin Larkin also died that day above the heights of Anzac Cove. Neither body was ever recovered. Their names are commemorated on the Lone Pine Memorial commemorating 4,934 Australian and New Zealand dead who have no known graves.

News of Larkin's death reached Australia in June 1915. A memorial service was held in St Mary's Cathedral to celebrate the life of this remarkable man and Australian. On 30 November 1915 the speaker of the New South Wales Legislative Assembly unveiled a commemorative plaque commemorating Sergeant Edward Rennix Larkin, member for Willoughby, and Colonel George Braund, Member for Armidale. The plaque reads: 'In time of peace they readily asserted the rights of citizenship. In times of war they fiercely protected them.'

This writer cannot think of a better man or Australian than Edward Larkin.

## International Caps
15 August 1903. Australia (3) 3 vs New Zealand (7) 22. Sydney Cricket Ground.

**Major Blair Inskip Swannell**
**1st Battalion, AIF**
**Died 25 April 1915**
**Aged 39**
**Forward**
**Eight Caps**

*'His conception of rugby was one of trained violence'*

Blair Inskip Swannell was born on 20 August 1875 in Weston Underwood, Buckinghamshire, the third of five children born to William and Charlotte Swannell. His father was a farmer and he was educated at home with his family before going up to Repton School in Derbyshire. On leaving school he attended the Thames Nautical Training College where he qualified as a second mate. Swannell first travelled to Australia in 1897 as a mate on a schooner and on returning to Britain joined the colors with 37th (Buckinghamshire) Company, 10th Battalion Imperial Yeomanry, serving with them during the Boer War. He quickly came to notice and, on 2 January 1902, was commissioned as a second lieutenant.

A larger than life character, Swannell claimed to have been in numerous adventures, many of which have never been substantiated. A forward who was known for his hard and frequently violent play, he was also infamous for his lack of hygiene and would often not wash his kit for months, making him unpopular with the other players.

Swannell first came to note playing for Northampton. In 1899, while playing for Northampton, he was invited to tour Australia with Matthew Mullineux's British Isles team and went on to play in seventeen matches of the tour, including three of the four tests.

He was re-selected for the 1904 tour of Australia and New Zealand, playing fifteen times, including all four test matches. During the match against New Zealand, Swannell's violent play was matched by the New Zealanders and he left the field at the end of the match bleeding and with two black eyes. His spirit, however, was undaunted.

Swannell fell in love with Australia and the Australians, and when the British team returned to England Swannell, together with David Bedell-Sivright and Doctor Sidney Crowther, decided to remain in Australia and try to make lives for themselves. He continued to play rugby, this time for Northern Suburbs whose ground was in Sydney.

In 1905 he was selected to play for Australia, even though he had already faced them as an opponent on six occasions. His first match was against New Zealand, Australia losing fourteen–three Australian Captain Herbert Moran disliked Swannell and his violent style of play, saying of him, 'Swannell was, for a number of years, a bad influence in Sydney football ... his conception of rugby was one of trained violence.'

It was the end of Swannell's playing career. Never daunted, he went on to coach youth and school level teams. As well as rugby he coached hockey, became vice president of Sydney Swimming Club and trained senior military cadets for surf life-saving exams. He especially excelled at St Joseph's College where he coached their rugby team to a number of championships. In 1909 he became Secretary of the Metropolitan Rugby Union and refereed from 1911 to 1914, becoming famous for his ability to control a game.

On the outbreak of the First World War Swannell took a commission in the Australian Imperial Force, later being promoted to major. On 25 April 1915, together with his men from D Company of the 1st Battalion, he landed in Anzac Cove and was immediately involved in the fighting for the infamous hill known as Baby 700. Pinned down by the Turks, Swannell was eventually shot in the head and killed.

He is commemorated at Baby 700 Cemetery in Gallipoli, Special Memorial. 10. He also has a memorial plaque on the wall at Weston-Underwood Church in Buckinghamshire. His next of kin at the time was given as Mrs Swannell, Castilian Terrace, Northampton, England.

## International Caps

22 July 1899. Australia (0) 0 vs Great Britain (3) 11. Exhibition Ground, Brisbane.

5 August 1899. Australia (0) 10 vs Great Britain (5) 11. Sydney Cricket Ground.

12 August 1899. Australia (0) 0 vs Great Britain 13. Sydney Cricket Ground.

2 July 1904. Australia 0 vs Great Britain 17. Sydney Cricket Ground.

23 July 1904. Australia (3) 3 vs Great Britain (0) 17. Exhibition Ground, Brisbane.

30 July 1904. Australia (0) 0 vs Great Britain (3) 16. Sydney Cricket Ground.

13 August 1904. New Zealand (3) 9 vs Great Britain (3) 3. Athletic Park, Wellington.

2 September 1905. New Zealand (3) 14 vs Australia (3) 3. Tahuna Park, Dunedin.

**29167 Gunner William George (Twit) Tasker**
**12th Field Artillery Brigade**
**13th Battalion & 116 Howitzer Battery**
**Died 9 August 1918**
**Aged 26**
**Fly-Half**
**Six Caps**

*'Well thought of and one of the best liked men in the Battery'*

William George Tasker was born in Condobolin, New South, Wales, the son of David Henry and Helene Tasker. He was educated at Newington College, Stanmore, New South Wales (1906–1911) and played fly-half for the college, captaining the first XV in 1911. In the same year he was selected for and captained the GPS Schools representative 1st XV, beating Sydney University. He remained in Sydney, completing his schooling before becoming a bank clerk (as well as studying for the law) whilst at the same time pursuing a rugby career.

In 1912, aged twenty, he made his debut for the Newtown Rugby Club in Sydney, later captaining the side. 'Twit' Tasker was described as about five feet six or eight inches high, rather stout build, fair complexion. He was also powerful and fast with one of the finest 'serves' in the game and was selected to play for the Australian side that toured North America in 1912 although he did not play in a single test. The squad was overwhelmed by hospitality and, lacking strong management, revelled in the social life and undergraduate antics of the college fraternity houses in which they were billeted. In what must be the worst record of any Australian touring team, the squad lost all their Canadian matches amongst five defeats. Tasker was the first Wallaby ever to be sent off the field. An incident occurred on the 1912 tour of the United States when Tasker's rough play upset an American referee.

Tasker made his test debut at Athletic Park (Wellington) on the 1913 tour of New Zealand and played in all three tests of that tour. The following year he made three further test appearances when the All Blacks toured Australia in a return series.

'Twit' Tasker enlisted as a gunner with 12th Field Artillery Brigade, on 26 January 1915 and departed Sydney on board HMAT A49 *Seang Choon* on 11 February 1915. He took part in the famous landings at Anzac Cove, Gallipoli, coming ashore late on 25

# England

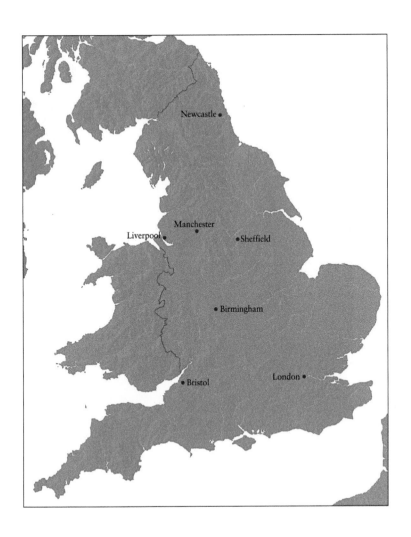

**Second Lieutenant Harry Alexander**
**1st Bn Grenadier Guards**
**Died 17 October 1915**
**Aged 36**
**Captain and Forward**
**Seven Caps**

*'Whatso'er thy hand findeth to do, do it with all thy might'*

Harry Alexander was born at Oxton, Cheshire on 6 January 1879. He was educated at Bromborough (1881 to 1891) and Uppingham school (1891 to 1897) before going up to Corpus Christi College, Oxford in 1897. He played in the Uppingham XV in both 1895 and 1896 as a forward. A good all-round athlete he also played cricket, hockey and fives for his school. He played for Oxford against Cambridge at Queen's Club in 1897 and 1898 winning the first by two tries to nil and losing the second by one goal and two tries to nil. He also played for Middlesex, for Cheshire for the North, for Birkenhead Park for the Barbarians and for Richmond. He went on to represent England seven times between 1900/02 scoring on his debut against Ireland and captaining England against Wales in January 1902. He ended his career as Captain of Richmond in 1905/06.

As well as excelling at rugby he was a county hockey player, a scratch golfer, a first class ice skater and a well-known Bandy player (a sort of ice hockey) in Davos Platz and St Moritz. More interestingly, he was also a professional singer, possessing a beautiful baritone voice. After leaving university he became a schoolmaster at Stanmore Park Preparatory School.

Harry had the reputation of being a hard-working forward and always being in the thick of it. He was also one of the most 'painstaking and punctilious' place kickers in the game.

He was commissioned in the Grenadier Guards on 23 July 1915 and went into training in both London and Marlow, travelling out to the front in October 1915. Like so many young officers of that tragic affair, he was killed by a shell on 17 October 1915, after only being at the front for thirteen days.

He is buried in the Arras Road Cemetery, Roclincourt, Pas de Calais, France (II, C.18).

# England

## International Caps

3 February 1900. England (7) 15 vs Ireland (4) 4. Athletic Ground, Richmond.

10 March 1900. Scotland 0 vs England 0. Inverleith.

5 January 1901. Wales (5) 13 vs England (0) 0. National Stadium, Cardiff.

9 February 1901. Ireland (5) 10 vs England (3) 6. Lansdowne Road, Dublin.

9 March 1901. England (0) 3 vs Scotland (15) 18. Rectory Field, Blackheath.

11 January 1902. England (8) 8 vs Wales (3) 9. Rectory Field, Blackheath. (Captain)

8 February 1902. England (3) 6 vs Ireland (0) 3. Welford Road, Leicester.

**5711 Corporal Henry Berry**
**1st Bn Gloucestershire Regiment**
**Died 9 May 1915**
**Aged 32**
**Forward**
**Four Caps**

*'Rugby football will always remember Berry of Gloucester'*

Henry (Harry) Berry was born on 8 January 1883, at 16 Alvin Street, Gloucester the youngest of ten children born to James and Hannah Berry. He attended St Mark's school and at the outbreak of the Boer war although only sixteen and too young for active service enlisted in the Gloucestershire Regiment. However, after his true age was discovered, he was posted to the 4th Militia Volunteers who were a home-based unit. When asked to guard Boer prisoners on St Helena, however, the entire battalion volunteered and departed England for the small island on board the RMS *Goth* in January 1900.

Duties on the island were not demanding and Harry found himself playing a lot of sports, being introduced for the first time to both rugby and hockey, two sports at which he excelled. At the conclusion of the war the battalion returned to England where Harry decided to continue his career with the Army, enlisting once again in the 1st Battalion Gloucestershire Regiment. He served with the Gloucestershire's in both Ceylon and India, becoming familiar with places like Lucknow, Umballa, Lahore and Bombay.

He continued to play rugby, captaining the D Company rugby team, who, under his guidance, remained unbeaten for five seasons. In 1909 Harry contracted malaria and was returned home. It looked like the end of his military career. He continued to play rugby, joining the Gloucester club at Kingsholm, first as a three-quarter and then as a forward (the position that suited him best). His obvious talents were quickly recognized and he was selected to play for Gloucester and then became reserve for England during the 1909 season.

In 1910 he married Beatrice Arnold and decided to become a publican, running the Red Lion and later the Stag's Head. His first child, George Berry, was born in 1911. On 15 January in the same year Harry was selected to play for England, making his debut against Wales. England won by six points to three, the first time England had beaten Wales since 1898. The following March Harry was in France playing at the Parc des Princes, Paris. England won by eleven points to three Harry scoring his debut try against the French. Harry ran over a try again in the Calcutta Cup match against Scotland on 19 March, England, finally defeating the Scots fourteen to five and Berry receiving much praise for his play and support. That season England won their first title since 1892 although, thanks to their draw with Ireland, they missed out on a first-ever grand slam. Despite having a first class season the England selectors stepped in once more and failed to select Berry again.

Despite this Berry continued to play rugby for Gloucester and was part of the 1910 county championship-winning side. Berry finally retired from rugby in 1913.

Still an Army reservist Harry was called up in August 1914. He was promoted to corporal before being sent to the front with the 1st Battalion Gloucestershire Regiment in February 1915. In May 1915 Harry, together with his regiment, was to take part on the Battle for Aubers Ridge. Unfortunately, the Germans were well prepared and the British plan was seriously flawed, as many were at the time. Berry went over the top with his battalion at four o'clock on 9 May 1915. They were met with a heavy withering machine-gun fire which cut the Gloucesters down like a scythe through corn. For the British the battle was a disaster. No ground was won and no positive effect achieved. During the attack the Gloucesters lost 262 men; Harry was amongst them, running forward to the end.

His body was never recovered and he is commemorated on the le Touret Memorial, Pas de Calais, France (Panel 17).

A month after his death his wife Beatrice gave birth to his second child, a daughter, Phyllis Irene.

## International Caps
15 January 1910. England (11) 11 vs Wales (3) 6. Twickenham.
12 February 1910. England 0 vs Ireland 0. Twickenham.
3 March 1910. France (0) 3 vs England (8) 11. Parc des Princes.
19 March 1910. Scotland (5) 5 vs England (5) 14. Inverleith.

**Major Henry Brougham**
**Royal Artillery**
**Died 18 February 1923**
**Aged 34**
**Wing**
**Four Caps**

*'Never did a man behave more bravely or bear an illness so well'*

Henry Brougham was born on 8 July 1888 at Wellington College, West Berkshire. He was educated at Wellington College where oddly, despite later playing for England four times, he failed to get into his school's XV, and didn't win his blue for rugby either, playing his club rugby for Harlequins. Brougham was one of those people, as many rugby players seem to be, who excelled at all sports. That said, and despite his ability at rugby, his best sport appears to have been rackets. He won the Public Schools Championship in 1907 and represented Great Britain in singles rackets at the 1908 London Olympics, winning a bronze medal. He was also the all comers' singles rackets champion winning the doubles' championship with B. S. Foster. Brougham was also a fine cricketer who got his blue at Oxford in 1911 (scored eighty-four runs against Cambridge). He went on to play for Berkshire County Cricket Club during the seasons 1905 to 1914 and for Minor Counties against South Africa in 1912.

He played rugby for England four times during the 1912 international season, scoring a try in England's eight nil defeat of Wales on his debut and another against Ireland in England's fifteen points to nil victory. Despite this, the match against France in April would be the last time Brougham would wear the England shirt.

Having joined the Army he was sent to France in 1915 with the Royal Artillery and rose to the rank of major before being seriously gassed in 1917 and invalided home. After suffering from the effects of the gassing for five years he finally succumbed to his injuries on 18 February 1923 at la Croix.

## International Caps
20 January 1912. England 8 vs Wales 0. Twickenham.
10 February 1912. England (3) 15 vs Ireland (0) 0. Twickenham.
16 March 1912. Scotland 8 vs England 3. Inverleith.
8 April 1912. France (0) 8 vs England (14) 18. Parc des Princes.

**Captain Arthur James (Mud) Dingle**
**6th Bn East Yorkshire Regiment**
**Died 22 August 1915**
**Aged 23**
**Wing**
**Three Caps**

*'We will never see his like again on the rugby field'*

Arthur James Dingle, (Mud) was born on 5 November 1891 in Hetton le Hole, County Durham. He was the son of the Reverend Arthur Trehane Dingle, Rector of Eaglescliff, and his wife Beatrice. He was educated at the Bow School, Durham before moving up to the Durham school itself. While at school he played three quarter, playing either at centre or on the wing.

After completing school he went up to Keble College, Oxford. While at Oxford his abilities on the field were quickly recognized and he was selected to play for Oxford turning out for them against Cambridge at the Queens Club on 12 December 1911. Oxford won a decisive victory by nineteen points to nil, Dingle managing to get the ball down between the posts. Despite this it was to be the only time he played for his university.

He went on to play for Richmond and Surrey before returning home and becoming a junior master at his old school in Durham. While back in Durham he played for Hartlepool Rovers and Durham. During the 1913/14 season he scored an impressive fifty-five tries and captained Hartlepool in 1914.

His fast pace and scoring abilities made him a certainty for an England cap and on 8 February 1913 he made his debut for England against Ireland in Dublin. Oddly, when he won his first cap, he was still at Oxford and gained his first international cap despite not being picked for the Oxford side in the same season. Unfortunately, 'Mud' didn't have the best of matches being described by *The Times* as 'Strong in defence, but was not altogether a success'. He was dropped for the rest of the international season.

Half way through the following season, however, Dingle was recalled for England. He played his first game against Scotland at Inverleith on 21 March 1914. Once again Dingle didn't have the best of games and once again *The Times* commented on it: 'At the opening of the game Dingle missed a pass with the goal line undefended 10 yards away.' However, despite a close game, England came out the victors, winning both the Calcutta Cup and the Triple Crown.

Dingle's final match was against France on 13 April 1914 at the Stade de Colombes. Despite rough play by the French and a hostile crowd, England came out victors by thirteen points to thirty-nine. Once again, however, Dingle was unable to reproduce his club form on the international stage and once again *The Times* picked this up, 'AJ Dingle was the weakest of the four. He failed to take the passes and was very slow getting into his stride.' This victory, however, gave England their second consecutive grand slam.

In September 1914 Dingle was commissioned in the 6th Battalion East Yorkshire Regiment. Despite there being few opportunities to play rugby Dingle did manage to turn out for the Barbarians against a team from the RAMC in April 1915. Dingle was promoted to captain before being shipped out to take part in the Gallipoli Campaign.

The 6th East Yorks landed at Suvla Bay on 6 August 1915. After landing the battalion was soon in action, driving the Turks off the small hillock of Lala Baba, but with many casualties. On 9 August Dingle's battalion was ordered to attack Scimitar Hill as a prelude to a larger attack the following day on the Teke Tepe ridge. Despite heavy casualties and against the odds the East Yorks took the hill. Later, however, they were forced to relinquish it for tactical reasons. Then, on 21 August, the battalion was ordered to take Scimitar Hill again. The attack failed disastrously. Arthur Dingle was at first reported missing, then assumed killed on 22 August 1915. His body was never recovered.

He is commemorated on the Helles Memorial Turkey (Panels 51 to 54).

His younger brother, Hugh John Dingle, was a doctor and died at Jutland while serving on HMS *Petard*.

## International Caps

8 February 1913. Ireland (0) 4 vs England (9) 15. Lansdowne Road, Dublin.

21 March 1914. Scotland (3) 15 vs England (3) 16. Inverleith.

13 April 1914. France (8) 13 vs England (13) 39. Stade Olympique, Paris.

**Lieutenant Colonel George Eric Burroughs Dobbs**
**Legion d'Honneur**
**Royal Engineers**
**Died 17 June 1917**
**Aged 32**
**Flanker**
**Two Caps**

*'He lived for only three or four hours after he was hit,*
*but his behaviour was a sample of that of a real soldier'*

George Eric Burroughs Dobbs was born on 21 June 1884 in Castlecomer, County Kilkenny, the son of Joseph and Mary. He was educated at St Stephen's Green School in Dublin where he played as a forward, winning a mathematical scholarship to Shrewsbury where he played goal for the first XI; he also rowed for his school and house. A keen sportsman, he captained their association football eleven, but that wasn't to be his game. By the time that he passed into the Royal Military Academy at Woolwich he had become a rugby union convert. Finishing his course in March 1904, he was gazetted as a second lieutenant in the Corps of Royal Engineers.

His love of rugby was great and he would play wherever and whenever he could. Amongst others he played for Devonport Albion, Devon, Plymouth Albion, and Llanelli. He quickly came to notice and on 13 January 1906 made his debut for England against Wales. It was a hard beginning for Dobbs. England hadn't beaten Wales since 1898 (although they did draw in 1904). The game went to Wales by sixteen points to three. Despite the heavy loss Dobbs retained his place in the England squad for the next match against Ireland. The match was played on 10 February 1906 in Leicester. Once again the English were outplayed and, although rallying in the second half, went down sixteen points to six. It was to be Dobbs's last international appearance.

It wasn't all doom and gloom for the forward. He was invited to join the Barbarians for their Easter tour to Wales. However, on the two occasions he played, he was on the losing side. On 13 April 1906 he lost to Penarth by five points to nil and, just to rub it in, lost to Cardiff the following day by thirty-eight points to nil. His final honour would come when he was selected to play for the Army against the Navy. The match was played at the Queen's Club, Kensington, and once again poor Dobbs was on the losing side. Although a hard fought match with the Army missing what would have been a winning kick in the last few moments, the Army went down by fifteen points to fourteen.

Dobbs was sent to France shortly after the outbreak of hostilities in 1914. Serving with the signal service, Royal Engineers during the BEF's retreat from Mons, not only was he promoted to captain, but also made a Chevalier of the Legion of Honour by the French. Serving with distinction, Dobbs was Mentioned in Despatches on three occasions. In 1916 he was promoted to lieutenant colonel and made Assistant Director of Signals. On 17 June 1917, near Poperinghe, Belgium, Dobbs was hit by a stray shell whilst surveying a new cable trench in the front line and died from his wounds later the same day.

He is buried in Lijssenthoek Military Cemetery, Poperinghe, West-Vlaanderen, Belgium (XIII, A. 5).

## International Caps

13 January 1906. England (3) 3 vs Wales (13) 16. Athletic Ground, Richmond.
10 February 1906. England (0) 6 vs Ireland (8) 16. Welford Road, Leicester.

**Lieutenant Commander Arthur Leyland Harrison VC**
**Royal Navy**
**KIA 23 April 1918**
**Aged 32**
**Forward**
**Two caps**

*'A national hero on every level'*

Arthur Leyland Harrison was born on 3 February 1886 in Torquay, Devon.

He was the son of Lieutenant Colonel A. J. Harrison of the Royal Fusiliers and his Wife Adelaide. He was educated at Dover College after which, on 15 May 1901, he commenced his naval career being posted to Britannia Royal Naval College, Dartmouth, as a cadet officer. He was then commissioned a sub lieutenant in 1906, with promotion to full lieutenant in 1908.

Having played rugby for his school as a forward, he went on to play for the Royal Naval College, Dartmouth and become a member of the Hampshire branch of the United Services from 1906 to 1914. He also played for the Hampshire county side between 1912 and 1914. His abilities on the rugby ground were quickly recognized and he was selected for his debut cap against Ireland at Twickenham on 14 February 1914. After a hard fought match, played in front of the King and prime minister, England came out on top seventeen points to twelve. Harrison certainly impressed the press (together with his namesake). *The Times* commented: 'the English forwards stiffened in the scrummage by the two Harrisons did better than against Wales.'

He next played for the Navy against the Army in their annual match on 7 March 1914 at the Queen's Club, the Navy going down by twenty-six points to fourteen. Although defeated, the Navy had fought hard and came close to turning the game around. Harrison played for England again on 13 April against France, defeating the French thirteen points to thirty-nine. This was to be Harrison's final match for England. The French victory secured England a second consecutive grand slam and Harrison was part of it, something any rugby player would be proud to know.

At the outbreak of the war Harrison, as a serving naval officer, was in the thick of the fighting almost at once. He took part in the battles of Heligoland Bight in 1914,

35

Dogger Bank in 1915 and on board HMS *Lion* at Jutland in 1916. For his service at Jutland, Harrison was Mentioned in Despatches (*London Gazette*, 15 September 1916) and was quickly promoted to lieutenant commander. In late 1917 Harrison volunteered for hazardous service, and was posted to HMS *Hindustan* at Chatham Docks in January 1918. After infantry training by the Middlesex Regiment, Harrison was posted to HMS *Vindictive* for the raid on Zeebrugge. It was during this raid that Harrison was to become a national hero.

Sir Roger Keyes created a plan that would block the port of Zeebrugge, making it impossible for the Germans to use it for their U-boats which were causing heavy losses to allied shipping. The raid was carried out on 23 April 1918, led by HMS *Vindictive* on board which Harrison had command of the Naval storming parties whose orders were to destroy the German shore batteries. At the beginning of the attack Harrison was hit by shrapnel which knocked him out and broke his jaw. Recovering, Harrison, despite his wounds, insisted on joining the mole assault team led by Lieutenant Commander Bryan Adams. On the mole, Harrison found Adams needed reinforcements, and sent him back to fetch marines. Harrison then led a party of men, including Able Seaman Albert McKenzie (also awarded the VC) with a Lewis gun. All the members of the assault team were killed or badly wounded. Able Seaman Eaves attempted to carry Lieutenant Commander Harrison's body back, but was wounded and taken prisoner.

The raid was only partially successful. Although the three blocking ships did scuttle themselves in the port, it was not in the planned positions and the port was only blocked for a few days. No fewer than eight Victoria Crosses were awarded for this brief action. Lieutenant Commander Arthur Leyland Harrison was one of them. The *London Gazette* of 14 March 1919 records the following:

For most conspicuous gallantry at Zeebrugge on the night of the 22nd–23rd April 1918. This officer was in command of the Naval Storming parties embarked in *Vindictive*. Immediately before coming alongside the Mole Lt Cdr Harrison was struck on the head by a fragment of shell which broke his jaw and knocked him senseless. Recovering consciousness he proceeded on to the Mole and took over command of his party, who were attacking the seaward end of the Mole. The silencing of the guns on the Mole was of the first importance, and though in a position fully exposed to the enemy's machine-gun fire Lt Cdr Harrison gathered his men together and led them to the attack. He was killed at the head of his men, all of whom were either killed or wounded. Lt Cdr Harrison, though already severely wounded and in great pain, displayed indomitable resolution and courage of the highest order in pressing his attack, knowing as he did that any delay in silencing the guns might jeopardize the main object of the expedition, i.e. the blocking of the Zeebrugge–Bruges Canal.

Harrison's body was never recovered and he is commemorated on the Zeebrugge Memorial, Brugge West-Vlaanderen, Belgium.

His VC was presented to his mother and then, in 1967, donated to the Britannia Royal Naval College, Dartmouth, where it is still on display.

In total four international rugby players have been awarded the VC. Arthur Harrison, Robert Johnson (21 October 1899), Thomas Crean (19 December 1901) and Fred Harvey (27 March 1917).

## International Caps

14 February 1914. England (6) 17 vs Ireland (7) 12. Twickenham.

13 April 1914. France (8) 13 vs England (13) 39. Stade Olympique Paris..

**Captain Harold Augustus Hodges**
**3rd Bn Monmouthshire Regt, attd 11th Bn South**
**Lancashire Regiment**
**Died 24 March 1918**
**Aged 32**
**Prop**
**Two caps**

*'Fast feet, safe hands, beloved by all'*

Harold Augustus Hodges was born on 22 January 1886 at the Priory, Mansfield Woodhouse, Nottinghamshire, the fifth of seven sons born to William and Augusta Hodges. He was educated at Roclareston School Nottingham, playing prop, before entering Sedbergh, in 1899. Sedbergh was a keen rugby playing school and Hodges's flair for the game was quickly recognized and he found himself playing for the first XV which he did for four years, captaining the team for the last two (he also played cricket for the school and captained the team for three years).

After leaving school Hodges went up to Trinity College, Oxford. His reputation preceded him and he was selected to play for Oxford in his first year at the university, obtaining his first blue against Cambridge on 12 December 1905 at the Queen's Club. Oxford was beaten by Cambridge and, more interestingly, Hodges played against his own brother, E. C. Hodges, a Cambridge blue.

Although he was on the losing side his performance still impressed and he was selected to play for England. His debut cap was against Wales at Richmond on 13 January 1906. Unfortunately the match was lost by sixteen points to three. Things didn't improve against Ireland a few weeks later (10 February 1906) and once again Hodges found himself on the losing side, this time sixteen points to six. It was to be the last time Hodges played for his country. Hodges continued to play rugby for Oxford, captaining the side in 1908. He also turned out for Midland Counties. After leaving Oxford, Hodges, a fluent French speaker, spent several months at the Sorbonne in Paris before returning to England in 1909 and becoming a master at Tonbridge School, being Senior House Tutor of School House. His sporting interests continued and he played both rugby and cricket (1912/13 season) for Nottingham.

and *The Times* commented, 'Kendall of Cheshire did not distinguish himself at half for England' Kendall was dropped by the selectors. Despite this he continued to play for the Barbarians during 1902, losing to both Swansea and Cardiff.

In 1903 Kendal was surprisingly back in the England team and this time as captain for their last match of the season against Scotland. Once again it was a hard fought match, its outcome not settled until towards the end with Scotland finally taking the victory by ten points to six. Scotland claimed the international championship and Calcutta Cup whilst England again picked up the wooden spoon. Although Kendall certainly played better it was to be his last appearance in an England shirt but he continued to play for both his club and county, Cheshire, turning out for them forty-five times. During this time he also found the time to get married to Katherine Minnie Bingham Kendall (neé Higginson).

Within twelve hours of the declaration of war, together with fellow international J. Baxter, he offered the Birkenhead Park RFC ground to the military and volunteered for service. He was commissioned in The Liverpool Scottish (1/10th King's Liverpool Regiment) as a lieutenant on 14 October 1914. Between 1914 and 1916 the Liverpool Scottish could boast at least seven rugby internationals as well as two former rugby captains of England and Scotland in their ranks. Kendall was posted to France on 1 November 1914. Like so many officers he endured the awful conditions and like so many officers he didn't last long, being shot and killed by a sniper on 25 January 1915.

He is commemorated in the Kemmel Churchyard Memorial, Heuvelland, West-Vlaanderen Belgium (Special Memorial 14).

## International Caps
9 March 1901. England (0) 3 vs Scotland (15) 18. Rectory Field, Blackheath.

11 January 1902. England (8) 8 vs Wales (3) 9. Rectory Field, Blackheath.

21 March 1903. England (3) 6 vs Scotland (7) 10. Athletic Ground, Richmond.

**357176 Lance Corporal John Abbott King**
**Yorkshire Hussars attd 1/10th (Liverpool Scottish)**
**Bn The King's Liverpool Regiment**
**Died 9 August 1916**
**Aged 32**
**Lock/Hooker**
**Twelve Caps**

*Yes, truly, well played, King; played indeed Sir.*

John King was born in Leeds on 21 August 1883, the son of John Abbott King and Mary Jane King, of Wharfedale Grange Farm, Ben Rhydding, near Ilkley, Yorkshire. He was educated at Giggleswick School, Settle, Yorkshire, between 1897 and 1899, getting his second XV colours with the school.

Emigrating to South Africa he played for Durbanville and Somerset West between 1903 and 1906. Retuning to England in 1906 he played for Headingley, Yorkshire and the Barbarians, as a forward. His speed, pluck and ability were quickly spotted and he was selected to play for England in every game the team played between 1910 and 1913, although he missed the England vs France game in Paris in 1912.

King was a farmer working on the slopes of Ben Rhydding, Yorkshire. Remarkably he stood only five feet five in height and was one of the smallest players ever to don the England shirt and described by many as the 'Pocket Hercules'. With the war only just started John King joined the Yorkshire Hussars on the morning of 9 August 1914, leaving his three sisters to bring in the harvest which they did with the help of the Yorkshire rugby team. At first he was turned down as he was an inch below the regulation height for the regiment. However as Jack himself put it, 'I've come purposely here to join the same regiment as my friend Lump, and I'm simply going to stick here until you take me in.' The regiment reconsidered and, on 12 August, he became a trooper.

Life in the Hussars wasn't all that Jack wanted and he saw little action. However, after a chance meeting with an old rugby playing friend, L. A. N. Slocock who was serving with the London Scottish, he managed to transfer to them. During this time he was also promoted to lance corporal and served with X Company The Liverpool Scottish.

However, his time with the regiment wasn't to be a long one. During the 8/9 August 1916 attack on Waterlot Farm, Guillemont, during the Battle of the Somme,

55th Division was stopped by fierce resistance on the first day. Two further attacks were made by the 1/10th Kings at 04.20 on 9 August, but again without success. Lance Corporal King was killed in action on this day at Guillemont. His old friend and fellow international Second Lieutenant L. A. N. Slocock, also of 1/10th King's, was killed on the same day.

King is commemorated on the Thiepval Memorial, Somme, France [Panels 1 D. 8B and 1 D8C]

## International caps

21 January 1911. Wales (5) 15 vs England (3) 11. St Helen's, Swansea.

28 January 1911. England (8) 37 vs France (0) 0. Twickenham.

11 February 1911. Ireland 3 vs England 0. Lansdowne Road.

18 March 1911. England (8) 13 vs Scotland (3) 8. Twickenham.

20 January 1912. England 8 vs Wales 0. Twickenham.

10 February 1912. England (3) 15 vs Ireland (0) 0. Twickenham.

16 March 1912. Scotland 8 vs England 3. Inverleith.

4 January 1913. England (3) 3 vs South Africa (3) 9. Twickenham.

18 January 1913. Wales 0 vs England 12. National Stadium.

25 January 1913. England (6) 20 vs France (0) 0. Twickenham.

8 February 1913. Ireland (0) 4 vs England (9) 15. Lansdowne Road.

15 March 1913. England (3) 3 vs Scotland (0) 0. Twickenham.

**Captain Ronald Owen Lagden**
**4th Bn King's Royal Rifle Corps**
**Died 3 March 1915**
**Aged 25**
**Number 8/Forward**
**One Cap**

*'He behaved with the utmost gallantry'*

Ronald Owen Lagden Born on 21 November 1889 in Maseru, Basutoland, on the border of present day South Africa. He was the son of Sir Godfrey Lagden KCMG and Lady Lagden, from Weybridge, Surrey. He was educated at Mr Pellat's School, Swanage before going to Marlborough College. Whilst at Marlborough he played rugby (half-back), cricket, hockey and rackets. After Marlborough he went up to Oriel College, Oxford, to read chemistry. While at Oxford, Lagden went on to win several blues in rugby, cricket, rackets and hockey.

He was selected to play for Oxford against Cambridge, the match taking place at Queen's Club on 11 December 1909 with the legendary Ronnie Poulton scoring five tries in a resounding Oxford victory. Lagden retained his place in the varsity squad the following year, once again meeting Cambridge at the Queen's Club, on 13 December. Although it was a much closer and much harder fought encounter, Oxford came out ahead by the thinnest of margins, twenty-three points to eighteen.

His ability in the two Oxford victories had not gone unnoticed and he was selected to play for England against Scotland on 18 March 1911. The match took place at Twickenham. Although the packs were evenly matched it was England who were to take the glory, defeating Scotland thirteen points to eight with Lagden kicking two conversions on his debut. England retained the Calcutta cup. For reasons unknown (some say he had a damaged knee but I'm not convinced by this) Lagden was never selected to play for England again.

Rugby wasn't Lagden's only sport as he was also a decent cricketer and, apart from playing for his university, turned out against Australia (1909), India (1911 – taking two wickets, one of them being their captain, Maharaja Bhupinder Singh of Patiala) and South Africa (1912). Lagden's final appearance for Oxford was at Lords in July 1912 where he scored sixty-eight runs and dismissed his brother Reginald, also a fine cricketer.

Back at Oxford Lagden turned out once again for the Oxford XV against Cambridge. The match was played on 12 December 1911 at the Queen's Club. Poulton was as brilliant as ever. Lagden played well and scored two conversations. *The Times* noticed, 'we have been hearing of the dashing play of Lagden ... but the best work is always anonymous'. Oxford were just too much for Cambridge and came out victors by nineteen points to nil.

After Oxford Lagden became a master at Harrow School (Headmaster's House). He continued to play rugby, this time for Richmond. As the lights went out all over Europe, Lagden enlisted in August 1914, joining the King's Royal Rifle Corps and being attached to the 4th Battalion. Posted to France, he was based in the St Eloi sector, some fifteen miles north of Neuve Chapelle on the Ypres salient. By 3 March 1915 Lagden was commanding a company, and was apparently well liked and respected. It was on that fateful day that Lagden led his men over the top in an attack on a heavily-defended German position. The well-sited machine guns did their work well. Of the 300 men involved in the attack 113 became casualties. Lagden was amongst the fallen. His CO later wrote to his family, 'He behaved with the utmost gallantry... A survivor who saw him fall says he was well away in front and the first man to fall ...'

His body was never recovered and he is commemorated on the Ypres (Menin Gate) Memorial (Panel 51 and 53).

## International Caps

18 March 1911. England (8) 13 vs Scotland (3) 8. Twickenham.

**Second Lieutenant Douglas (Danny) Lambert**
**East Kent Regiment (The Buffs)**
**KIA 13 October 1915**
**Aged 32**
**Wing**
**Seven Caps**

*'He gave me more confidence than anyone I have ever played with'*

Douglas (Danny) Lambert, was born in Cranbrook on 14 October 1883 and educated at St Edwards, Oxford, before moving up to Eastbourne College. After a brief period playing footballer (inside right) he converted to rugby union in 1900.

A large man who was both strong and fast with a good kicking foot, Lambert joined the formidable Harlequins club. Initially he played forward for their A team before being finally selected for the first XV in 1905 as a wing three-quarter. This was largely due to outpacing the normally speedy Adrian Stoop and pushing him into touch just before he could score.

He was later selected for the Barbarians' traditional Easter tour to Wales in 1906. Unfortunately, Barbarians' form was poor and he was on the losing side in his three matches against Penarth, Cardiff and Plymouth. Lambert was finally selected to play for England against France. The match was played at Richmond on 5 January 1907 and Lambert was outstanding, scoring no fewer than five tries in England's forty-one to thirteen drubbing of the French. Even *The Times* was impressed by Lambert's performance: 'Seizing the opportunity, D. Lambert did the actual scoring with almost unerring accuracy.'

The score equalled the world record established by Scotland's George Lindsay in their match against Wales in 1887, and would not be bettered until the 1995 World Cup when All Black Marc Ellis scored six tries against Japan. Once again the unfathomable minds of the selectors stepped in and he was dropped from the squad for the rest of the international season.

Despite this, Lambert continued to play for Harlequins and once again joined the Barbarians for their Easter tour to Wales. This time he was on the winning side against Penarth and Devonport but lost to Cardiff. In 1908 Lambert was back in the England squad and he scored another try against France in England's defeat of the French, followed by two defeats against Wales and Ireland (where he scored two conversions). He played against the touring Australians for the London division losing by a try to nil (24 October 1908). On 2 October 1909 he played for Harlequins against Richmond at the new Twickenham Stadium. Once again Lambert was outstanding. As the *Sportsman* commented, 'The Harlequins soon added another try, the ball coming down the line to Lambert who sprinted away from everyone.' Lambert added a conversion to this try, Harlequins finally coming out on top fourteen points to ten.

The 1911 international season saw Lambert back in favour with the national selectors once again. He played three times, losing to Wales at Swansea, hammering the French once again, this time at Twickenham thirty-seven points to nil, Lambert scoring two tries, five conversions and two penalties, a total of twenty-two points. This record for points scored in one match was to remain until 1990 when Simon Hodgkinson scored twenty-three in a fifty-one point to nil victory over Argentina. Lambert's final match was a defeat by Ireland in Dublin, three points to nil. By now Lambert had seven caps; he was to get no more. His last 'international' was against the South African touring side for a London Division team, which they lost by twelve points to eight.

With war being declared in August 1914 Lambert was commissioned in the 6th Battalion of The Royal East Kent Regiment (The Buffs). In December 1914 he was posted to France with his battalion, but not before marrying his childhood sweetheart, Joyce, at West Brompton and getting her pregnant. Lambert was to take part in the battle of Loos, which commenced on 25 September 1915. The battle, saw the first use by British troops of poison gas and the first use of tunnelling by companies of the Royal Engineers. Although the British did gain some ground it wasn't much. However they did hang onto it despite heavy German counter-attacks. On the 13 October, the day before Lambert's birthday, the British tried one more time to see if they could break through. The Buffs went over the top, led by their officers, to be met by a withering fire from German machine-gun positions. The battalion lost 400 men in just a few minutes, advancing just one hundred yards before being forced to halt. Lieutenant Douglas Lambert was one of the dead. He has no known grave and is commemorated on the Loos Memorial (Panels 15 to 19).

His son was born just two months after his death.

## International Caps

5 January 1907. England (13) 41 vs France (13) 13. Athletic Ground, Richmond.

1 January 1908. France (0) 0 vs England (6) 19. Stade Olympique, Paris.

18 January 1908. England (8) 18 vs Wales (15) 28. Ashton Gate, Bristol.

21 March 1908. Scotland (7) 16 vs England (10) 10. Inverleith.

21 January 1911. Wales (5) 15 vs England (3) 11. St Helen's, Swansea.

28 January 1911. England (8) 37 vs France (0) 0. Twickenham.

11 February 1911. Ireland (3) vs England (0). Lansdowne Road, Dublin.

**Lieutenant Alfred Frederick Maynard**
**Howe Battalion, Royal Naval Division**
**Died 13 November 1916**
**Aged 22**
**Hooker**
**Three Caps**

*'A man impossible to stop when he had the ball'*

Alfred Frederick Maynard was born on 23 March 1894 in Anerley, Kent, the son of the late W. J. Maynard, the probate registrar of Durham (from 1903) and former international association footballer, and his wife Annie, of 'Hillsborough', West Bay Road, Bridport, Dorset. He was educated at Seaford School and Durham School, playing hooker for both. He was also captain of the school cricket, fives, and gymnastics teams and went on to play rugby for both Durham City and Durham County. On finishing school he went up to Emmanuel College, Cambridge, and whilst there not only won his blue (1912 / 13) but also turned out for Harlequins.

Maynard played his debut against Oxford on 10 December 1912. The Cambridge team overwhelmed Oxford, taking the match ten points to three. It was Cambridge's first win since 1903. He played again the following year this time scoring a memorable try the light blues took the match by thirteen points to three. *The Times*, commenting on his size and strength, wrote:

> At any rate the Oxford man who finally ran at him full tilt (Maynard) in order to push him over the line a foot away, bounced off him without causing him any inconvenience or preventing him from scoring a try in the corner.

Almost certainly because of this victory, Maynard was selected to make his debut for England against Wales on 17 January 1914. The match was played at Twickenham with England pulling off a hard fought and close ten points to nine victory. Maynard had another good game and once again *The Times* commented, 'To ... AF Maynard go the scanty laurels of the English forwards'. On 14 February Maynard returned to Twickenham to take on the Irish. Both the king and the prime minister were in attendance. Outplayed at first, the Englishmen dug in and came out eventual winners by seventeen points to twelve. Maynard's final match was played on 21 March 1914

He was called up on 5 August 1914 and, as a member of the Oldham Territorials, known as the 1/10th Battalion Manchester Regiment, went to train with them at Bury. The battalion was then sent to Egypt and thence to the Hell Hole known as Gallipoli, taking part in the landings on 25 April 1915. Billy Nanson was to meet his end during the Third Battle of Krithia. The attack took place on 4 June 1915. The 10th went over the top and, after doing well initially, the fighting intensified and the battalion was forced back to its original lines. Lieutenant Bleakley of D Company described some of what happened:

> Sixty men from 188, made it to the Turkish trenches, after being relieved two days later, only four made it back; some days later the company strength was only twenty-seven men. The casualties to the battalion are estimated at eighty-two killed, 320 wounded.

Sergeant Nanson was last seen advancing down a Turkish trench singlehandedly clearing it with his rifle and bayonet and calling back to his men 'Come on Lads, let's shift them' like the forward he was. He was later reported missing in action. However, with no news he was declared dead presumed killed thirteen months later on 4 June 15. Like thousands of other men his body was never recovered.

He is commemorated on the Helles Memorial, Turkey (Panel 158 to 170).

## International Caps

5 January 1907. England (13) 41 vs France (13) 13. Athletic Ground Richmond.
12 January 1907. Wales (13) 22 vs England (0) 0. St Helen's, Swansea.

**Lieutenant Francis Eckley Oakeley**
**Royal Navy**
**Died 1 December 1914**
**Aged 23**
**Scrum Half**
**Four Caps**

*'The Warrior Sportsman'*

Francis Eckley Oakeley was born on 5 February 1891, the fifth son of the Reverend James Oakeley, the Vicar of Holy Trinity, Hereford, and his wife Frances. He was educated at the Hereford Cathedral School before entering the Royal Naval College at Osbourne on the Isle of Wight when he was thirteen. Two years later he moved up to Dartmouth to complete his training. Leaving Dartmouth in 1908 at the tender age of seventeen he became a midshipman.

While still a junior officer, Oakeley was selected to play for the Royal Navy against the Army on 14 March 1911 at the Queen's Club. The Navy lost by thirteen points to twenty-two, not the best of debuts but his fortunes would change. In November of the same year Oakeley was promoted to sub lieutenant. He played scrum-half for both the Navy and the United Services, as well as fencing, another sport he excelled at. Selected again to play for the Navy against the Army on 2 March 1912, he was determined that this time there would be no mistake. Under the watchful eyes of King George V and the Prince of Wales, the Navy emerged as victors by sixteen points to eight. On 30 October that year Oakeley turned out for the Combined Services against the visiting South Africans. The tourists came out on top by a whisker, eighteen points to sixteen.

On 1 March 1913 Oakeley was once again selected for the Navy side that took on the Army. As usual he was on the winning side the Navy, coming out victorious by eighteen points to eight. His contribution to the game so impressed the England selectors that, just two weeks later on 15 March 1913, he made his debut against Scotland at Twickenham. England came out on top by three points to nil assuring England their first ever grand slam. *The Times* was full of praise for the young naval officer, 'F. E. Oakeley did the "donkey work" with mechanical accuracy, passing at a nice pace well in front of his partner.'

Oakley then transferred to HMS *Dolphin* to begin his training in submarines and was later promoted to full lieutenant.

Selected once again in 1914 to play for the Navy against the Army, although this time on the losing side, the Army defeating the Navy by sixteen points to twenty-four, this brought his Naval caps to four. He was capped again against Ireland, Scotland and France as England not only retained the championship but also took a second successive grand slam.

Posted to the D-class submarine HMS *D2* on 28 August 1914, he took part in the battle of Heligoland Bight, one of the first naval actions of the war and a great British success. A few months later, however, the submarine was to suffer a double tragedy. On 23 November *D2*'s Commanding Officer, Lieutenant Commander Jameson, was swept overboard in bad weather and despite a valiant search disappeared presumed lost. *D2* was sent out on patrol once more on 25 November, this time with Lieutenant Commander Head in charge. During this patrol she disappeared and was never seen again. Later it was discovered that the sub had been rammed by a German patrol boat whilst patrolling off Borkum on the German-Dutch border. Oakeley's death was a tragedy to both the Navy and the sport of rugby. We can only guess what heights he might have achieved.

He is commemorated on the Portsmouth Naval Memorial, Hampshire, England (Panel 1).

## International Caps

15 March 1913. England (3) 3 vs Scotland (0) 0. Twickenham.

14 February 1914. England (6) 17 vs Ireland (7) 12. Twickenham.

21 March 1914. Scotland (3) 15 vs England (3) 16. Inverleith.

13 April 1914. France (8) vs England (13) 39. Stade Olympique, Paris.

**Lieutenant Ronald William Poulton-Palmer**
**4th Bn Royal Berkshire Regiment**
**Died 5 May 1915**
**Aged 25**
**Captain/Centre**
**Seventeen Caps**

*'It is indeed, hard to say "farewell" to such a man'*

Ronald William Poulton-Palmer was born on 12 September 1889, the second son and fifth child of Professor (Zoology) Edward Bagnall Poulton and Mrs Emily Palmer Poulton of Wykeham House, Oxford. His mother was the daughter of George Palmer, co-founder of the Huntley and Palmers biscuit-making business in Reading, which Ronnie joined upon coming down from university. In 1914 he was left a significant fortune by his uncle, G. W. Palmer, on condition that he changed his surname to Palmer. As a result, he is often referred to in print as 'Poulton Palmer' or 'Poulton-Palmer.'

He was educated at the Dragon School, Oxford (1897–1903), where he played wing/centre, before going to Rugby School (1903–08) and, later, Balliol College Oxford (1908-11). A first-rate athlete, while at Rugby he won the athletic cup three times, played in the first XV (captaining the side in his last year) and was also in the cricket XI. He was in the Varsity XV while at Oxford, playing for them three times between 1909 and 1911, being on the winning side on all three occasions. He also played hockey for Oxford between 1909 and 1911. Given his record for Oxford he soon came to the attention of the England selectors and was chosen to make his debut against France on 30 January 1909 at Welford Road, Leicester. England won twenty-two points to nil. Palmer was only nineteen years old. It was to be his first of seventeen caps for England.

As well as England and Oxford, Palmer also played for Harlequins, Liverpool and representative sides East Midlands and London. Although a brilliant player, he also had an unorthodox style which could at times concern the selectors who would look to a 'safer' pair of hands and overlook him. This might also explain why he was overlooked for the varsity team in December 1908. That wasn't true, however, of Adrian Stoop captain of Harlequins who spotted Palmer's potential from a very early stage and selected him to play in the first team. Stoop was also influential with the England

Trotter Hermon-Hodge Bt, the Unionist candidate. He continued playing rugby for Old Merchant Taylors on their ground at the Old Deer Park, Richmond, captaining the side, and also captained the RFU tour of Argentina in 1910, the international match being won, three – twenty-eight but no cap was awarded. It was the South American nation's inaugural test.

Despite being a pacifist he joined up in August 1914 at the outbreak of the war. At first he enlisted into the ranks of the Honourable Artillery Company but in December 1914 was gazetted into the West Riding Regiment before finally transferring to the 18th Battalion King's Royal Rifle Corps. He was later appointed to the General Staff as an aide de camp to the General Officer Commanding, 41st Division which is not surprising, especially as he was cousin to the battalion's founder, Major Sir Herbert Raphael, MP for South Derby. Raphael died at Remy on 11 June 1917 of wounds received at Messines Ridge on 7 June. A friend of his, Captain Eric White described what happened:

> There were four of us together, our GSO 3, my servant, and myself. We were just leaving the dug-out, and John and my servant were in front. I was immediately behind them ... the shell burst only a few feet in front of us. I was more or less knocked over, and when I recovered myself my servant ran to me saying he was hit. I took him into the dug-out to see if he was bad or not. After some moments I heard John say in a perfectly natural voice, 'Will you come here a minute?' I went outside and found him lying near the door, obviously wounded ... I don't think he suffered much pain ... he never made a murmur or complaint.

It was later discovered that his wounds were far worse than had been first thought. Although he was operated upon it was all too late.

Raphael is buried in Lijessenthoek Military Cemetery, Poperinghe, West-Vlaanderen, Belgium (Grave XIII, A. 30).

## International Caps

11 January 1902. England (8) 8 vs Wales (3) 9. Rectory Field, Blackheath.

8 February 1902. England (3) 6 vs Ireland (0) 3. Welford Road, Leicester.

15 March 1902. Scotland (0) 3 vs England (6) 6. Inverleith.

14 January 1905. Wales (11) 25 vs England (0) 0. National Stadium. Cardiff.

18 March 1905. England 0 vs Scotland 8. Athletic Ground, Richmond.

2 December 1905. England (0) 0 vs New Zealand (9) 15. Crystal Palace, London.

13 January 1906. England (3) 3 vs Wales (13) 16. Athletic Ground, Richmond.

17 March 1906. Scotland (3) 3 vs England (3) 9. Inverleith.

22 March 1906. France 0 vs England (22) 35. Parc des Princes.

**Major Reginald (Reggie) Oscar Schwarz MC**
**6th Bn King's Royal Rifle Corps**
**Died 18 November 1918**
**Aged 43**
**Fly-Half**
**Three Caps**

*'He possessed the most supreme modesty and self-effacement'*

Reginald Oscar Schwarz was born on 4 May 1875 at Lee in London and educated at St Paul 's school before going up to Christ's College, Cambridge. After leaving university he became a member of the Stock Exchange (1911) and a partner in the firm of Parsons and Henderson. A good all-round athlete, he excelled at both rugby and cricket. While at Cambridge he managed to get his blue in rugby playing for Cambridge against Oxford on 13 December 1893 playing halfback. *The Times* was impressed and wrote of Schwarz 'Oxford heeled the ball out, but before any of their side could hold it Schwarz raced up'. Despite Schwarz's best efforts, however, Cambridge went down by one try to nil.

Schwarz played his club rugby for Richmond and Middlesex. Although his career had a bright start it wasn't until 10 April 1897 that he was finally picked to play for the Barbarians against Hartlepool Rovers. This time he was on the winning side, defeating Hartlepool by fourteen points to nine. Despite this Schwarz had to wait two years 15 February 1899) to be selected again, this time against Stade Français, thirty-three points to nil. The size of the victory and Schwarz's part in it came to the notice of the English selectors and he was picked to play his England debut at against Scotland on 11 March 1899. It was the final international in one of England's poorest seasons and they went down by five points to nil giving them the wooden spoon.

Schwarz was recalled to the England squad a year later, being selected to play against Wales at Cardiff on 5 January 1901. Despite playing at least as well as the Welsh, England went down by thirteen to nil. England's efforts were not lost on the selectors and Schwarz retained his place for the following game against Ireland at Lansdowne road on 8 February. Despite playing well once again, in what was considered a bad-tempered game, England lost by ten points to six and were left holding the wooden spoon. It was Schwarz's last appearance for his country. He continued to play for the Barbarians joining their Easter tour to Wales, being on the losing side against Newport by nine points to three before drawing with Cardiff six points all.

Not only did Schwarz have a sporting career in rugby but also in cricket. He played first for Oxfordshire before moving to Middlesex in 1901. In 1902 he emigrated to South Africa, working for Sir Abe Bailey, the well-known diamond dealer, as his personal secretary. While there he turned out for the Transvaal and toured England with the South African cricket team in both 1904 and 1907, forging a reputation as being one of the finest bowlers of his age. He went on to win twenty caps for South Africa, before retiring in 1912. By then he had taken 398 wickets at a fine 17.58 average, and in Tests he took fifty-five at 22.60. Despite his poor batting – he passed fifty only twice in first-class cricket – Schwarz did make a century: 102 in a non-Test game against an England XI at Lords in 1904.

In August 1914 Schwarz served in German South West Africa and was Mentioned in Despatches for his part in it. After Africa Schwarz joined the 6th Battalion King's Royal Rifle Corps and joined them in France in January 1916. By 11 November 1918 Schwarz had been wounded twice, become a major, been given a staff job and was not only Mentioned in Despatches once again, but also won a Military Cross in the New Year's Honours list of 1917 (gazetted 1 January 1917).

He was taken ill the day after the Armistice and died of influenza a week later on 18 November 1918. He is buried in Étaples Military Cemetery (Grave XLV, A. 4).

## International Caps
11 March 1899. England 0 vs Scotland 5. Rectory Field, Blackheath.
5 January 1901. Wales (5) 13 vs England (0) 0. National Stadium, Cardiff.
9 February 1901. Ireland (5) 10 vs England (3) 6. Lansdowne Road, Dublin.

**Second Lieutenant Lancelot Andrew Noel Slocock**
**1/10th Bn (Liverpool Scottish) Liverpool**
**Regiment**
**KIA 9 August 1916**
**Aged 29**
**Captain/Forward**
**Eight Caps**

*'Among the greatest of them there is no doubt Noel Slocock holds a high place'*

Lancelot Andrew Noel Slocock was born on 25 December 1886 at Wooton Wawen, Warwickshire, the third son of the Reverend F. H. Slocock and his wife Judith. He was educated at Marlborough College where he not only played in the rugby XI but in both the cricket and hockey XIs. On leaving school he continued his rugby with Liverpool (Secretary Liverpool RFC 1907/1908) and also turned out in the North vs South match. Having come to notice during this match he was selected to make his England debut against the visiting South Africans in December 1906 at the Crystal Palace. However, and almost comically, he was the subject of a clerical error and his place was taken by a medical student at Guy's Hospital called Arnold Alcock. Although Alcock was a decent club player he was no international. Alcock eventually became a GP in Gloucester and later President of Gloucester RFC. Slocock did face South Africa in their next match, against Lancashire, a county for whom Slocock would eventually win fourteen caps. Slocock scored a try in this match, although the South Africans went on to win.

He was selected again, to play France at Richmond on 5 January 1907. This time the selection process seemed to work well and Slocock ran out with the rest of the team. Although the French played well they were hammered forty-one points to thirteen with Slocock playing well and scoring a try. Because of his performance against France, Slocock was selected to play for England for the rest of the 1907 international season. He next appeared against Wales on 12 January at Swansea. This time it was England's turn to get thumped twenty-two points to nil. However Slocock still played well and impressed *The Times*, 'the English forwards had periods of relative success, and the efforts of some of them, notably L.A.N. Slocock.... deserved a better fate'. His next match was against Ireland in Dublin. The match was played on 9 February and although England's performance had certainly improved, and Slocock scored yet again, they still

**Surgeon James Henry-Digby (Bungy) Watson**
**Royal Navy (HMS *Hawke*)**
**Died 15 October 1914**
**Aged 24**
**Centre**
**Three Caps**

*'Selected for Scotland, played for England'*

James Henry Digby Watson was born on 31 August 1890 in Southsea, the son  of
Engineer Captain J. H. Watson RN and Mrs E. V. Watson, of Westwood, Helensburgh,
Scotland. He was educated at King's college, Canterbury (1899-1906 where he played
centre for the school's first XV. From here he went up to Edinburgh Academy (1906-08)
once again playing centre in the first XV. It was while he was at the Academy that he
picked up his nickname 'Bungy' after asking for a rubber in the King's school slang. After
leaving school in 1908 he decided to become a doctor and was accepted at Edinburgh
University to read medicine (1908-13). Whilst at the university he became the university
middleweight boxing champion and represented Scotland in the long jump.

He played his rugby for Edinburgh Academicals, participating in one of their most
successful periods. He was invited to play for the Barbarians on their Christmas tour
of Wales in 1911. Watson played two matches, losing to Cardiff on 26 December
by nineteen points to nil and Newport by fifteen points to six on the 27th. Despite
these losses Bungy was invited to play for them again the following year, firstly on 30
December 1912, against Leicester, when he was once again on the losing side fifteen
points to eleven. Watson captained the Academicals during the 1912 and 1913 season
and was also selected as the three-quarter reserve for Scotland (although never capped).
He travelled to Wales with the Barbarians once again for their Easter tour in 1913 and
was again defeated in both games he played in, losing by ten points to nil to Cardiff (22
March) and by eight points to nil to Swansea (24 March). In fact, Watson was defeated
in all five games he played for the Barbarians.

Having completed his studies and become a doctor Watson moved to London. In
London he played for both Blackheath and London Hospitals. He was soon spotted by
the England selectors who chose him to make his debut against Wales on 17 January
1914. The match was played at Twickenham, England coming out ahead by a whisker,

ten points to nine. *The Times*, mentioning Watson's contribution to the game, noted, 'JHD Watson could do very little by [his] straight forward methods, so keen was the tackling'.

Watson missed England's next match against Ireland but was reinstated for the game against Scotland at Inverleith on 21 March. Although England was the better side, the Scots refused to be overwhelmed and almost pulled the game back. However, in another close fought match, England were the victors by sixteen points to fifteen. Watson was kept in the side for the match against France to be played in Paris on 13 April. This time it was a far more simple affair with England coming out easy victors by thirteen points to thirty-nine. It was in this match that Watson was to score his one and only international try. Once again *The Times* commented on Watson's performance: 'of the three-quarter backs JHD Watson and Lowe were the best ... Watson made some mistakes at first, but was on top of his form in the second half'. With this win England retained the international championship with a second successive Grand Slam. Despite England's success it was Watson's last appearance in an England shirt.

Watson joined the Royal Navy at the outbreak of war and was posted to HMS *Hawke*, an armoured cruiser and one of the oldest ships in the Royal Navy as a temporary surgeon. On 15 October 1914 the Hawke was on patrol with her sister ship HMS *Theseus* in the North Sea some sixty miles from Aberdeen when she was attacked by the German submarine U9, commanded by Leutnant Otto Weddigen, one of the German navy's most able captains. In September 1914 he had sunk three cruisers, *Aboukir*, *Hogue* and *Cressy*, in only a few hours. The *Hawke* was hit amidships close to her magazine by a torpedo. She blew up and sank in less than eight minutes with the loss of over 500 men.

Surgeon James Watson is commemorated on the Chatham Naval Memorial,

## International Caps
17 January 1914. England (5) 10 vs Wales (4) 9. Twickenham.
21 March 1914. Scotland (3) 15 vs England (3) 16. Inverleith.
13 April 1914. France (8) 13 vs England (13) 39. Stade Olympique, Paris.

**8074 Private Arthur Wilson**
**12th Bn Royal Fusiliers**
**Died 1 July 1917**
**Aged 30**
**Olympian**
**Forward**
**One Cap**

*'Upheld the tradition of sporting excellence'*

Arthur James Wilson was born in Newcastle upon Tyne on 29 December 1886, the son of Henry and Emily. After attending the Glenalmond School, Wilson moved up to the Camborne School of Mines to begin his professional education. Arthur just loved the game and couldn't seem to find enough games to play in. He played for Camborne, Camborne School of Mines and Camborne Students. His energy and ability came to notice and he was selected to play for Cornwall, a county he was capped for seventeen times.

In the 1908 County Championship campaign Cornwall reached the final for the first time in the county's history. Their opponents were Durham. They were an impressive side and this was to be their nineteenth consecutive appearance in the final. The match was played on 28 March 1908 at Redruth, Cornwall, in front of a crowd of 17,000 people. As with football, finals are funny things and, despite Durham's previous and impressive victories, Cornwall played the better rugby and Durham were beaten seventeen points to three.

In 1908 the Olympic Games were held in London. Many international teams such as South Africa and New Zealand didn't really take the games seriously as a 'rugby event' and withdrew from the Olympics while arguments broke out amongst the home international teams. The entire event looked like it might dissolve into a farce especially when even France, previous Gold Medal winners, withdrew and left the way free for Australia to win the gold medal by default. To try and avoid this Cornwall, as the county champions, were approached by the Rugby Union to take up the challenge and not allow Australia a walk over.

Cornwall arrived to play the Olympic final at a near-empty White City Stadium on 26 October 1908. Cornwall didn't play well and Australia was by far the better side, eventually winning the Gold Medal by thirty-two points to three. Despite losing the gold medal it wasn't the end of Wilson's career and he was selected to play for England against Ireland on 13 February 1909 at Lansdowne Road. This, however, was to be his only international cap.

With his studies complete Wilson travelled the world, working as a mining engineer and tea/coffee planter until returning home at the outbreak of war to enlist. He enlisted into the Royal Welsh Fusiliers as a private, later being promoted to corporal. Unfortunately, like so many before him, Wilson was killed in Flanders on 1 July 1917 at the third battle of Ypres (Passchendaele).

Arthur Wilson is commemorated on the Ypres (Menin Gate) Memorial, Ieper, West-Vlaanderen, Belgium (Panels 6 and 8).

## International Caps
13 February 1909. Ireland (5) 5 vs England (0) 11. Lansdowne Road, Dublin.

**Captain Charles Edward Wilson Légion d'Honneur**
**Queen's Royal West Surrey Regiment**
**Died 17 September 1914**
**Aged 43**
**Forward**
**One Cap**

*'Played the game to his very last breath'*

Charles Wilson was born on 2 June 1871 in Fermoy, County Cork, Ireland. He was the son of Major General F. E. E. Wilson CB and Mrs Wilson and was educated at Dover College where he was in the first XV and played forward. On leaving school he decided to join the Army, getting a place at the Royal Military College Sandhurst in July 1892. He passed out in July 1896 and was commissioned into 1st Battalion, The Queen's (Royal West Surrey Regiment). He played as a forward for Blackheath, the Army and Surrey. Then on 5 February 1898 he was selected to play for England against Ireland at the Athletic Ground, Richmond. Although Wilson worked hard and solidly in the scrum, England went down by six points to nine. There can be little doubt that he would have earned further caps had his career not been cut short by a broken leg while playing in the South vs North game. However, some have cast doubt on this explanation stating that although he certainly broke his leg in the match it was before he won his first and only international cap.

During the campaign in South Africa (the Boer War) he served on the staff, taking part in the Relief of Ladysmith, Colenso, Spion Kop, Vaal Kranz, Tugela Heights and Pieters Hill, as well as further operations in Natal. He was Mentioned in Despatches (*LG* 29 July 1902) and in August 1901 was promoted to captain. After returning home he continued to play for Blackheath before being posted to India and being forced to give up his honorary secretaryship of the Army Rugby Union. During this period he also found time to marry (Mabel) and have two sons.

At the outbreak of hostilities in 1914 he went to France with his regiment as captain and adjutant, landing at le Havre on 13 August 1914. He was awarded the Legion d'Honneur before being killed in action on 17 September 1914 on the River Aisne.

He is buried in Paissy Churchyard, Aisne, France (Grave 2).

## International Caps
5 February 1898. England (0) 6 vs Ireland (6) 9. Athletic Ground, Richmond.

# France

Paris

Nantes

Lyon

Bordeaux

Nice

Marseille

**Lieutenant Rene Emile Henri Boudreaux**
**103ème Régiment d'Infanterie**
**Died 8 September 1915**
**Aged 34**
**Prop**
**Two Caps**

*'A vaincre sans péril, on triomphe sans gloire.'*
*'To win without risk is a triumph without glory.'*

René Boudreaux was born on 27 November 1880 in Paris. He played his rugby for Sporting Club Universitaire de France as a prop forward.

He was capped for France twice during the 1910 Five Nations' Championship, the first year France was allowed into the competition. He made his first appearance at St Helen's, Swansea, against Wales on New Year's Day. Wales simply overwhelmed the French defeating them by forty-nine points to fourteen. His second and final match in a French shirt was against Scotland at Inverleith played on 22 January 1910. Once again France were out-played and defeated by twenty-seven points to nil.

During the First World War Rene Boudreaux was recalled to serve with the French Army. He was killed in action on 8 September 1915 near Auberive while serving as a lieutenant with the 103rd Infantry Regiment of the 7th Infantry Division.

He is commemorated on the following:

Monument Commémoratif du Loze R.I. in Aubèrive
Plaque Commémorative, Èglise Saint Séverin Paris.
Plaque Commémorative 1914–1918 Espci Paris.

**International Caps**
1 January 1910. Wales (21) 49 vs France (14) 14. St Helen's, Swansea.
22 January 1910. Scotland (11) 27 vs France (0) 0. Inverleith.

**Private Second Class Marie Jean-Baptiste Joseph Anduran**
**226ème Regiment d'Infanterie**
**Died 2 October 1914**
**Aged 32**
**Hooker**
**One cap**

*L'ile Des Braves*
*None but the brave*

Marie Jean-Baptiste Joseph Anduran, better known as Joé Anduran, was born on 24 April 1882 in Bayonne. A picture gallery employee by profession, he played hooker (number 8) for SCUF (Sporting Club Universitaire de France). He won the Championship as captain of SCUF second team in 1912 and in 1913 was a member of the first team that lost the final in the National Championship in Paris. Anduran also served as club secretary between 1908 and 1914.

In 1910 France was admitted into the Five Nations' Championships for the first time. During a trip to Swansea on 1 January 1910 the French side found themselves with a problem when the team manager, Charles Brennus, discovered he only had fourteen players to travel to Wales with. To make sure they played with a full side, Anduran was invited to join the side at the last minute as a result of a chance meeting with French Rugby Union Secretary Cyril Rutherford who was desperate to field a full side. As a result Anduran played for France against Wales. It was to be his only appearance for his country.

At the outbreak of war Anduran joined the 226th Infantry Regiment as a private soldier. He didn't survive long and was shot in the heart and killed at Bois Bernard on 2 October 1914. He left behind a wife and two children, Jacqueline, six, and five-month-old Jean.

His name is engraved on the monument to the dead of Bayonne.

## International Caps
1 January 1910. Wales (21) 49 vs France (14) 14. St Helen's, Swansea.

81

**Lieutenant Maurice Jean-Paul Boyau**
**Medaille Militaire, Chevalier de la Legion**
**d'Honneur**
**Officier de la Legion d'Honneur**
*Service Aéronautique*
**Died 16 September 1918**
**Aged 30**
**Flanker**
**Six Caps**

*'Qui craint de souffrir, il souffre déjà de ce qu'il craint.'*
*'He who fears suffering is already suffering that which he fears'.*

Maurice Boyau was born on 8 May 1888, in Mustapha (Algeria). In 1905 he was the co-founder of Club Sportif de Bretigny (Association Football) who have played at Stade Maurice Boyau, along with US Dax Rugby Club, since 1922. He also played forward for Stade Bordelais Université Club. Between 1 January 1912 and 24 March 1913 he represented France six times, against Ireland (twice), Wales (twice) Scotland and England, captaining the side twice, but being on the losing side on every occasion, although they were unlucky against Wales. It has to be remembered that France were not the international side they are today and were in the infancy of their international development, having only been allowed to play in the Five Nations in 1910.

Whilst not playing rugby, Boyau was a professional soldier and was serving with the 144ème Régiment d' Infanterie when war was declared. However, he was quickly transferred to the 18ème Escadron du Train des Equipages as a driver before starting training as a pilot with the Service Aéronautique at the end of 1915. He received his pilot's brevet on 28 November 1915 and was assigned as an instructor at Buc. In September 1916 he finally managed to get to the front, transferring to Escadrille N77 (later *SPA77*) as a corporal. The squadron was known as 'les Sportifs' because of the great number of athletes in its ranks.

A natural and aggressive pilot, Boyau originally flew Nieuports, his paint scheme featuring a rather flamboyant serpentine dragon writhing the length of the plane's white fuselage. Later the squadron was given Spads and it was in the Spad that Boyau did most of his damage. In the spring of 1918, Boyau pioneered the use of air-to-air rockets. He had several rocket tubes affixed to the inner set of inter-plane struts of his Spad XIII. However, I could find no record as to how successful these were during the First World War.

His first victory came on 16th March 1917 when he shot down a German Aviatik that had just shot down another member of the squadron, Lieutenant Havet. On 3 June 1917, together with his friend Gilbert Sardier, he shot down his first observation balloon. Two days later he downed another. Thus started his reputation as a 'balloon buster'. On the latter occasion he had trouble with his plane and was forced to land on the German side of the line. However, before the German infantry could reach him, he managed to repair it and fly away, being fired at by the Germans all the way. Shooting down a balloon on the face of it anyway sounds like an easy task but it wasn't; they were very heavily defended and many pilots thought it suicide to even go near a balloon, never mind attack one.

Boyau was awarded the Medaille Militaire on 27 June 1917 after his fifth victory. His citation read:

> Pursuit pilot of audacious bravery. Three times cited in orders, and has to his credit an aircraft and a balloon. On the 5th of June he destroyed another balloon. Forced to land in enemy territory, he repaired his plane and flew back over the lines at 200 metres altitude, under fire of enemy machine guns.

He was promoted to sous lieutenant, and was made a Chevalier de la Legion d'Honneur after his tenth victory in September 1917. On 29 May 1918 he shot down two German Albatross scouts, followed by an observation balloon.

The awards kept coming. He was given the Rosette d'Officier de la Legion d'Honneur after his 28th victory in July 1918. The citation read:

> Pilot of remarkable bravery whose marvellous physical qualities are put to use by his most arduous spirit and fights at great heights. Magnificent officer with an admirable spirit of self-sacrifice, facing each day with the same smiling desire for new exploits. He excels in all branches of aviation; reconnaissance, photography in single-seaters, bombardments at low altitudes, attacks on ground troops, and is classed among the best pursuit pilots. He has reported twenty-seven victories, the last twelve in less than one month. Has downed sixteen balloons and eleven planes. Has the Medaille Militaire and Chevalier de la Legion d'Honneur for feats of war. Eleven citations.

Maurice Boyau achieved thirty-five victories (twenty-one of them balloons) before being shot down and killed himself on 16 September 1918 by Leutnant Georg von Hantelmann of Jasta 15. Hantelmann went on to claim twenty-five victories himself before the end of the war. He was credited with shooting down Boyau as his fourteenth victory. Boyau was the fifth most successful French fighter pilot of the war. He was to have been presented on the 29th with a diamond and platinum Legion of Honour cross bought by a halfpenny subscription made among all the athletes of France.

A stadium of one of his former clubs, Dax, France is named after him, Stade Maurice Boyau, to commemorate this remarkable fighting Frenchman.

## International Caps

1 January 1912. France (6) 6 vs Ireland (11) 11. Parc des Princes.

20 January 1912. Scotland (13) 31 vs France (3) 3. Inverleith.

25 March 1912. Wales (6) 14 vs France (8) 8. Rodney Park, Newport.

8 April 1912. France (0) 8 vs England (14) 18. Parc des Princes.

27 February 1913. France (0) vs 8 Wales (3) 11. Parc des Princes.

24 March 1913. Ireland (8) 24 vs France (0) 0. Mardyke, Cork.

**Lieutenant Jean Jacques Conilh De Beyssac**
**Tank Commander AS 15 Tank Group**
**Died 13 June 1918**
**Aged 28**
**Prop/Lock**
**Five Caps**

*'Celui qui a bon coeur n'est jamais sot.'*
*' He who has a good heart can never be a fool.'*

Jacques Conilh de Beyssac was born on 12 April 1890 in Cauderan. He played flanker/ lock for Stade Bordelais Université. Stade Bordelais toured Great Britain in 1908/09, and played Richmond although he is not on the team sheet. It is very likely that, in order to get a game, he walked across to Rosslyn Park to pick up a game with them as his name appears in the rugby club's minutes. He played for France five times between January 1912 and April 1914, being on the losing side each time.

At the outbreak of war he was commissioned as a lieutenant, serving with the 81er Artillerie Lourde. In October 1917 he became a lieutenant in 501st Tank Regiment (AS15). Despite being heavily involved in the war he still found time to play in a French Military XV against the Anzacs at the la Cipale Stadium at Vincennes, playing for a Coupe de la Somme. However, he was on the losing side once more.

AS 15 was in action for the first time on 11 June 1918 during the Battle of Méry. In all, 173 Schneiders and Saint Chamonds were used by General Mangin during this counter-attack on Courcelles-Epayelles, Méry, Belloy and Lataule. The attack went in at 9.40am from Montgerain wood in the direction of Méry. At approximately two o clock, Beyssac's tank was hit by three shells and destroyed. Beyssac and three members of his crew were seriously wounded in the explosions. He died on 13 June from wounds received in action while in a military ambulance (hospital) at St Remy.

Commemorated on the Monument aux Moets at Cussac – Fort-Médoc.

## International Caps

1 January 1912. France (6) 6 vs Ireland (11) 11. Parc des Princes
20 January 1912. Scotland (13) 31 vs France (3) 3. Inverleith
1 January 1914. France (3) 6 vs Ireland (0) 8. Parc des Princes
2 March 1914. Wales (13) 31 vs France (0) 0. St Helen's, Swansea.
13 April 1914. France (8) 13 vs England (13) 39. Stade Olympique, Paris.

**Lieutenant Marcel Henry Burgun CdG**
**Service Aéronautique**
**Died 2 September 1916**
**Aged 25**
**Fly-Half, Wing, Centre**
**Eleven Caps**

*'Le courage, c'est l'art d'avoir peur sans que cela paraisse.'*
*'Courage is the art of being frightened and not showing it.'*

Marcel Henry Burgun was born on 30 January 1890 in St Petersburg, Russia. He read engineering at the École Centrale Paris, which is one of the oldest and most prestigious engineering schools in France. He played his rugby for Racing Club de France, playing centre. He represented France eleven times between March 1909 and April 1914, playing fly-half, losing ten and winning one against Scotland on 2 January 1911, France's first ever international victory. He also played in the last game against England before the outbreak of the First World War.

He entered military service in 1910 and with the outbreak of war in August 1914 was made a sub-lieutenant in an artillery regiment. After being involved in some fierce fighting in defence of his country and Paris, Burgun was transferred at his request to the French air corps in 1915. His brother had been killed in action and he was out for revenge. He joined Escadrille MF50, later Escadrille N38, Aviation Militaire. At first he flew as an observer, pinpointing targets for artillery but became restless and, in September 1915, applied to become a fighter pilot. He was promoted to the rank of lieutenant ingénieur and was credited with at least one victory (probably as an observer), a German Aviatik, which was forced to land on 5 August 1915. He also received three citations for bravery, including a posthumous Croix de Guerre.

He set out on his last patrol on 2 September 1916, flying a Nieuport XVII south of Aubérive. He was attacking one German aircraft when he was shot down by a German escort fighter and killed.

He is buried in the Cimitière de Mont Frenet, la Cheppe, Marne, France.

## International Caps

20 March 1909. Ireland (8) vs France (0) 8. Lansdowne Road. Dublin.

1 January 1910. Wales (21) 49 vs France (14) 14. St Helen's Swansea.

22 January 1910. Scotland (11) 27 vs (0) 0. Inverleith.

28 March 1910. France (3) 3 vs Ireland (8) 8. Parc des Princes.

2 January 1911. France (11) 16 vs Scotland (8) 15. Stade Olympique, Paris.

28 January 1911. England (8) 37 vs France (0) 0. Twickenham.

1 January 1912. France (6) 6 vs Ireland (11) 11. Parc des Princes.

20 January 1912. Scotland (13) 31 vs France (3) 3. Inverleith.

1 January 1913. France (3) 3 vs Scotland (8) 21. Parc des Princes.

25 January 1913. England (6) 20 vs France (0) 0. Twickenham.

13 April 1914. France (8) 13 vs England (13) 39. Stade Olympique, Paris.

**Corporal Paul Henri Descamps**
**246ème Régiment d'infanterie**
**Died 27 June 1915**
**Aged 31**
**Flanker/Lock**
**One Cap**

*'Fuyez un ennemi qui sait votre défaut.'*
*'Fear the enemy who knows your weakness.'*

Paul Henri Descamps was born on 14 January 1884 in Paris. He played as a forward for Racing Club de France. Although he only appeared in one international it was an important one: he was a member of the team that beat Scotland by sixteen points to fifteen at the Stade Olympique in Paris. It was France's first international victory and Descamps kicked two match-winning conversions. Despite this, for some reason he never played for France again.

At the outbreak of war he became a corporal in the 246ème Régiment d'Infanterie and was killed in action at Souchez on 27 June 1915.

## International Caps
2 January 1911. France 11 16 vs Scotland 8 15 Stade Olympique, Paris.

# France

**Lieutenant Julien Dufau**
**7th Regiment of Colonial Infantry**
**Died 28 December 1916**
**Aged 28**
**Centre/Wing**
**Four Caps**

*'Le monde appelle fous ceux qui ne sont pas fous de la folie commune.'*
*'Mad are labelled those who do not take part in the common madness.'*

Julien Dufau was born on 16 or 18 February 1888 in Biarritz, the son of Adolph and Mary Chastain who resided at Vaureal Street, Biarritz. Dufau enlisted in the army on 5 October 1905 joining the 49th Infantry Regiment. However, he left the army after only a few years in June 1911 and returned to Biarritz. He played wing for Biarritz Stadium and was eventually selected to play for France in the Five Nations games of 1912. He played in all four matches, being on the losing side in each but he did score a try against Ireland on 1 January 1911 during his debut and another against England on 8 April 1911 in front of his home crowd. On 18 March 1908 he married his childhood sweetheart, Laurence Dupau, in Biarritz.

He was mobilized by the French army on 2 August 1914, joining the 7th Regiment of Colonial Infantry in Bordeaux. In December 1915 he was promoted to lieutenant before leaving with his regiment for Niger in January 1916. On arrival he was given command of a section of the Senegal Camel Corps. His first mission was to deal with the German and Turkish backed Senoussi revolt, which he did with ruthless efficiency.

In October 1916 he became involved in the fighting at Zurrika, Amazalla and Tarbardak. His commanding officer the unusually named (for the war), Captain Bosch said of him:

His activity, energy, together with an unusual strength allowed him to quickly become a méhariste like the Tuareg have little known ... It would be advisable that we have such leaders in charge of our camel units .

In December 1916 Father de Foucauld (a former French army officer who became an explorer, geographer, Catholic religious and linguist and who was beatified in 2005), was murdered during the Kaossen rebellion, an attempt to drive the French out of

Niger. On 28 December 1916 Lieutenant Dufau, while returning from a mission in Bilma, was ambushed near a place called Tin Taboraq (about twenty kilometres east of Agadez). Two-thirds of the column was killed in the ambush and Lieutenant Julien Dufau was captured, together with four other members of the column. He, together with the other prisoners, was later beheaded on the orders of Tegama Sultan of Agadez and their heads exhibited for several days before the palace of the sultan. It took until March 1917 before the bodies of the patriotic Frenchmen could be recovered and given a decent burial in the Agadez French cemetery.

Lieutenant Dufau received three citations in 1916, two in military orders. He was promoted to Knight of the Legion of Honour posthumously in 1920. The new French fort at Agadez was named after the brave lieutenant and called Fort Dufau.

## International Caps
1 January 1912. France (6) 6 vs Ireland (11) 11. Parc des Princes.
20 January 1912. Scotland (13) 31 vs France (3) 3. Inverleith.
25 March 1912. Wales (6) 14 vs France (8) 8. Rodney Park, Newport.
8 April 1912. France (0) 8 vs England (14) 18. Parc des Princes.

**Private Paul Dupré**
**2ème Classe, 4ème Zouaves**
**Died 31 March 1916**
**Aged 27**
**France**
**Flanker**
**One Cap**

*'Celui qui obéit est presque toujours meilleur que celui qui commande.'*
*'He who obeys is almost always better than he who commands.'*

Paul Dupré was born on 29 June 1888 in Gagny He played hooker for Racing Club de France but only played once for France – against Wales – in 1909, France going down forty-seven points to five. During the First World War he served with the 2ème Classe 4ème Zouaves and was captured by the Germans. He died in Altengrabow, Germany on 31 March 1916 in a prisoner of war camp which held 20,000 Russian, Belgian, British and French soldiers.

Commemorated on Monument aux Morts 914–1918 in Gagny.

**International Caps**
23 February 1909. France (0) 5 vs Wales (9) 47. Stade Olympique, Paris.

**Sous Lieutenant Albert Victor (Eutrope)**
**6ème Colonial Infantry**
**Died 26 May 1915**
**Aged 27**
**Flanker**
**One Cap**

*'À cœur vaillant rien d'impossible.'*
*'Nothing is impossible for a willing heart.'*

Albert Eutropius was born on 10 January 1888 in Cayenne, French Guiana and moved to Paris in 1910 where he played prop for Sporting Club Universitaire de France (SCUF), playing position number eight and flanker. He played in two championship of France finals, one in 1911 and again in 1913 and was selected for France to play Ireland on 24 March 1913, France winning by twenty-four points to nil. It was to be his one and only appearance for his country. He was also only the second black man ever to wear French colours.

When the war broke out Eutropius was a colonial administrator in Africa and was immediately commissioned as a second lieutenant before being mobilized to fight in the Cameroon. He was shot through the head and killed on 26 May 1915 at Masseng, Cameroon.

He was buried at N'Gato and his name inscribed on the monument to the dead of Cayenne.

## International Caps
24 March 1913. Ireland (8) 24 vs France (0) 0. Mardyke, Cork.

**Captain Marc Giacardy**
**6ème Régiment d'Infanterie**
**Died 20 August 1917**
**Aged 36**
**Fly-Half, Flanker, Half back**
**One Cap**

*'À l'impossible nul n'est tenu.'*
*'No one is bound to do the impossible.'*

Marc Giacardy was born on 15 February 1881 in Gironde, Bordeaux. He played his rugby for Stade Bordelais (SBUC), who were champions of France six times between 1899 and 1909, and was also captain in 1909. Giacardy was selected to represent France on one occasion against Wales in 1907, a match France lost quite heavily forty-one points to thirteen. During the 1911/12 French rugby club final between Stade Toulousain and Racing Club de France he refereed the match (which wasn't uncommon at the time). Outside rugby he worked as a journalist.

During the war he served as a captain with the 6ème Régiment d'Infanterie and was killed in action on 20 August 1917 at the head of his men, leading an attack at Mormont farm near that hell on earth, Verdun.

Commemorated on Livre d'Or du Lycée de Bordeaux.

## International Caps
5 January 1907. England (13) 41 vs (13) 13. Athletic Ground, Richmond.

**Lieutenant Pierre Guillemin**
**Died 17/18 August 1915**
**Aged 27**
**Prop/Lock**
**Eleven Caps**

*'Quand le vin est tiré, il faut le boire.'*
*'Once the first step is taken there's no going back.'*

Pierre Guillemin was born on 13 September 1887 in Brougils. He played his rugby for Racing Club de France. An architect by profession, he was one of the outstanding French players of his day and turned out eleven times for France between 1908 and 1911, being on the losing side on ten occasions but being part of the French Squad that beat Scotland on 2 January 1911, their first-ever international victory.

During the war he served as a lieutenant with the 23ème Regiment d'Infanterie. He was killed in action on 18 August 1915 at Belleville-sur-Meuse.

## International Matches

1 January 1908. France (0) vs England (6) 19. Stade Olympique, Paris.

2 March 1908. Wales (17) 36 vs France (4) 4. National Stadium.

30 January 1909. England (10) 22 vs France (0) 0. Welford Road, Leicester.

20 March 1909. Ireland (8) 19 vs France (0) 8. Lansdowne Road, Dublin.

1 January 1910. Wales (21) 49 vs France (14) 14. St Helen's, Swansea.

22 January 1910. Scotland (11) 27 vs France (0) 0. Inverleith.

3 March 1910. France (0) 3 vs England (8) 11. Parc des Princes.

28 March 1910. France (3) 3 vs Ireland (8) 8. Parc des Princes.

2 January 1911. France (11) 16 vs Scotland (8) 15. Stade Olympique, Paris.

28 January 1911. England (8) 37 vs France (0) 0. Twickenham.

25 February 1911. France 0 vs Wales 15. Parc des Princes.

**Sergeant Maurice (Putty) Hédembaigt**
**89ème Regiment d'Infanterie**
**Died 5 August 1918**
**Aged 27**
**Scrum-half/Half Back**
**Three Caps**

*'À tout seigneur tout honneur.'*
*'Honour to whom honour is due.'*

Maurice Hédembaight (nickname Putty) was born on 3 February 1891 in Auglet. A house painter by trade, he played his rugby for Aviron Bayonnals who were established in 1904 and played from their ground, Jean Dauger, Bayonne, in the Basque region of France. During the 1912/13 season Bayonnals beat SCRUF in the final of the French Rugby Union Championship thirty-one to eight at the Stade Yves-du-Manoir. He was selected to play for France three times, twice in 1913 and again in 1914, being on the losing side each time. A fine all-round athlete, he was also Basque Coast long-jump champion.

During the war he served as a sergeant with 89ème Régiment d'Infanterie (although some records show him with the 19th Infantry). He was killed in action on 5 August 1918, at the ferme du Goulet (Marne).

Commemorated on Monument aux Morts, Bayonne.

### International Caps
1 January 1913. France (3) 3 vs Scotland (8) 21. Parc des Princes
11 January 1913. France (5) 5 vs South Africa (11) 38. le Bouscat, Bordeaux.
2 March 1914. Wales (13) 31 vs France (0) 0. St Helen's. Swansea.

**Corporal Emmanuel Francois Iguinitz**
**49ème Régiment d'Infanterie**
**Died 20 September 1914**
**Aged 24**
**Hooker**
**One Cap**

*'Qui va lentement va sûrement.'*
*'Slowly but surely.'*

Emmanuel Iguinitz was born on 9 December 1889 in Bayonne. He was an artisan jeweller and watchmaker by trade and played his rugby for Aviron Bayonnals who won the French Rugby Union First Division Championship during the 1912/13 season, beating SCUF 31-8 on 20 April 1913 at the Stade Olympique, Yves-du-Manoir. It was a triumph for such a new club. A French newspaper commented:

> The crowd chaired Bayonne's players off the pitch while former French Captain Gaston Lane wrote in *l'Auto* (nowadays *l'Equipe*) that they had played with 'stunning brio, amazing audacity and, most of all, staggering skill'.

By the end of 1914 several of the players from that match were dead. Five of Bayonne's victorious 1913 team died in the First World War: Emmanuel Iguinitz, Jean Francois Poeydebasque, Emmanuel Iguinitz and Maurice Hédembaigt.

Iguinitz served with the 49ème Régiment d'Infanterie during the war and was killed in action on 20 September 1914 at Craonne.

Commemorated on Monument aux Morts, Bayonne.

## International Caps
13 April 1914. France (8) 13 vs England (13) 39. Stade Olympique, Paris.

**Lieutenant Medical Officer Daniel Ihingoue**
**633ème Bataillon de Tirailleurs**
**Died 16 April 1917**
**Aged 28**
**Centre**
**Two Caps**

*'La caque sent toujours le hareng.'*
*'What's bred in the bone will come out in the flesh.'*

Daniel Ihingoue was born on 13 January 1889 in Ilharre (Pyrénées Atlantiques). As a medical student he played his rugby for Bordeaux Etudiants Club as well as Biarritz Stade, Biarritz Olympique and Stade Rochelais. He was selected to play for France twice, once against Scotland and the other against Ireland in January 1912, being on the losing side on both occasions.

During the war he served with the 633ème Bataillon de Tirailleurs, a colonial Senegalese infantry unit, as its medical officer (there seems some confusion as to whether he was a doctor or a medical student. It changes from account to account ). He was awarded the Croix de Guerre with Vermeil Star for bravery before being killed in action on 16 April 1917 at Craonne on the Aisne.

Commemorated on Plaque Commémorative Faculte de Medecine, Bordeaux.

### International Caps
1 January 1912. France (6) 6 vs Ireland (11) 11. Parc des Princes.
20 January 1912. Scotland (13) 31 vs France (3) 3. Inverleith.

**Lieutenant Henri Isaac**
**5ème Regiment Mixte de Zouaves et Tirailleurs**
**Service Aéronautique**
**Died 20 June 1917**
**Aged 34**
**Full Back**
**Two Caps**

*'Ce n'est pas à un vieux singe qu'on apprend à faire la grimace.'*
*'There's no substitute for experience.'*

Henri Isaac was born on 7 May 1883 in Basse-Terre, Guadeloupe and played his rugby for Racing Club de France, also known as RCF (founded on 20 April 1882 under the name Racing Club) where he played full back. Racing Club de France was one of the inaugural teams in the French Championship. They won the championship in 1892, 1900 and 1902 and were runners up in 1893 and 1912. He was selected to play for France twice, on both occasions against England, in 1907 and 1908; France lost both games.

During the war Henri served as a lieutenant with 5ème Regiment Mixte de Zouaves et Tirailleurs. Later he joined the French flying corps and was killed on 20 June 1917 in an accident, possibly as a result of his parachute failing to open.

## International Caps
5 January 1907. England (13) 41 vs France (13) 13. Athletic Ground, Richmond.
1 January 1908. France (0) 0 vs England (6) 19. Stade Olympique, Paris.

**Sergeant Jean Pierre Henri Lacassagne**
**2nd Squadron Aviation Group C46**
**Died 14 September 1918**
**Aged 34**
**Scrum-half**
**Two Caps**

*'Ce n'est pas la vache qui crie le plus fort qui fait le plus de lâit.'*
*'Talkers are not doers.'*

Jean Pierre Henri Lacassagne was born on 27 December 1883 in Viella. After leaving school at Viella he attended Lycée Montaigne Bordeaux High School where he played rugby for his school. After a business venture in South America he finally settled in Nantes and played his rugby for Stade Bordelais, at scrum-half, and was on the champion team of France in 1904, 1905, 1906, 1907 as well as being a finalist in 1908. He won two caps for France, one against New Zealand (Parc des Princes) on 1 January 1906 and the other against England (Athletic Ground, Richmond) on 5 January 1907. It was to be his last appearance for France.

During the war Lacassagne first served with the 59th Infantry Regiment and was wounded with them in Avocourt Wood in 1915. On recovering, he was posted to the Air Weapons' School at Cazaux. From there he went to 46th Squadron of the 2nd Aviation Group as a gunner. His ability and gallantry quickly came to note and he received his first citation for bravery:

'Excellent gunner, courage and coolness above all praise, seriously injured in a fight against 15 enemy aircraft, bravely overcame his pain.'

Despite his bravery, life in the flying service was short and on 14 September 1918 in the sky over Saint Benedict (Haute-Marne), he was shot and killed during a major dogfight with a German squadron. During the fight he was hit in the chest. However, despite his wound, he continued with the fight. Unfortunately, he was hit again, this time in the head, and killed.

Two months later Lacassagne received his second citation for bravery:

Excellent gunner of courage and remarkable address. On 14th September 1918, during a bombing mission he was involved in a particularly valiant fight against

7 enemy planes shooting one of his opponents down. Shortly afterwards he was shot down himself.

After the war, the first sports ground in the village of Viella was named after him. He is buried in Cimetiére de la Misericorde, Nantes.

## International Caps
1 January 1906. France (3) 8 vs New Zealand (18) 38. Parc des Princes.
5 January 1907. England (13) 41 vs France (13) 13. Athletic Ground, Richmond.

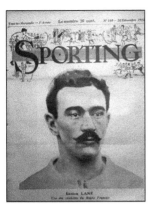

**Private Gaston Ernest Lane**
**1ère Classe, 346ème Regiment d'Infanterie**
**Died 23 September 1914**
**Aged 31**
**Wing/Centre**
**Sixteen Caps**

*'Qui se fait brebis le loup le mange.'*
*'Nice guys finish last.'*

Gaston Lane was born on 31 January 1883 in Paris. An engineer by profession he first played wing/centre for AS Bois-Colombes, then Cosmopolitan Club of Paris before finally representing Racing Club de France. An intelligent man and good all-round sportsman, he also played football and wrote for the French sports magazine *Sporting*. He was selected to play for France on no fewer than sixteen occasions, starting with New Zealand on 1 January 1906 and finishing with Scotland on 1 January 1913. He was on the losing side for all but one of these matches, that against Scotland on 2 January 1911, France's first international victory. He was the first French player, together with Marcel Communeau, to be capped ten times for France.

During the war he served with 1ère Classe, 346ème Regiment d'Infanterie and was killed in action on 23 September 1914 at Stenay/Lerouville.

He is commemorated on Monument aux Morts du Cimetiére Ancien, Le Raincy.

## International Caps

1 January 1906. France (3) 8 vs New Zealand (18) 38. Parc des Princes.

22 March 1906. France (0) 8 vs England (22) 35. Parc des Princes.

5 January 1907. England (13) 41 vs France (13) 13. Athletic Ground, Richmond.

1 January 1908. France (0) 0 England vs (6) 19. Stade Olympique, Paris.

2 March 1908. Wales (17) 36 V France vs (4) 4. National Stadium, Cardiff.

30 January 1909. England (10) 22 vs France (0) 0. Welford Road, Leicester.

23 February 1909. France (0) 5 vs Wales (9) 47. Stade Olympique, Paris.

20 March 1909. Ireland (8) 19 vs France (0) 8. Lansdowne Road, Dublin.

1 January 1910. Wales (21) 49 vs France (14) 14. St Helen's, Swansea.

3 March 1910. France (0) 3 vs England (8) 11. Parc des Princes.

2 January 1911. France (11) 16 vs Scotland (8) 15. Stade Olympique, Paris.

28 February 1911. France 0 vs Wales 15. Parc des Princes.

1 January 1912. France (6) 6 vs Ireland (11) 11. Parc des Princes

25 March 1912. Wales (6) 14 vs France (8) 8. Rodney Road, Newport.

8 April 1912. France (0) 8 vs England (14) 18. Parc des Princes.

1 January 1913. France (3) 3 vs Scotland (8) 21. Parc des Princes.

L'ÉQUIPE DE FRANCE FONDÉE PAR L'U. S. F. S. A.

*De gauche à droite au troisième rang debouts* : Cyril RUTHERFOND (arbitre de touche) ; LAFFITTE ; THEVENOT ; BOUDREAUX ; MAURIAT ; GUILLEMIN ANDURAN ; HOURDEBAIGHT ; MASSÉ.
*Au second rang assis* : MENRATH ; BURGUN ; LANE ; HOUBLAIN ; BRUNEAU.
*Au premier rang assis* : MAYSSONNIÉ ; MARTIN.

**Sergeant Jean Aime Larribau**
**12ème Régiment d'Infanterie**
**Died 31 December 1916**
**Aged 27**
**Wing/Scrum-half**
**Seven Caps**

*'Il faut laisser le passé dans l'oubli et l'avenir a la Providence.'*
*'One must forget about the past and leave the future up to Providence.'*

Jean Larribau was born on 2 March 1889 at Anglet. He played his rugby for CA Perigueux Biarritz (CAP) and Biarritz Olympique. He was renowned for his long passes. A journalist who watched him play commented, 'He was a small man endowed with a exceptional pass which permitted his fly-half to stand 25-30 meters from the scrummage.' Lattibua played for France on seven occasions between 1 January 1912 and 13 April 1914 but was on the losing side on each occasion.

During the war he served as a sergeant with 12ème Regiment d'Infanterie and was killed in action on 31 December 1916 at Poivre on the Verdun sector of the Western Front.

He is commemorated on Monument aux Morts, Biarritz and buried at Verdun National Necropolis Glorieux, Tomb 2816.

## International Caps
1 January 1912. France (6) 6 vs Ireland (11) 11. Parc des Princes.

20 January 1912. Scotland (13) 31 vs France (3) 3 Inverleith.

25 March 1912. Wales (6) 14 vs France (8) 8 Rodney Parade, Newport.

8 April 1912. France (0) 8 vs England (14) 18. Parc des Princes.

1 January 1913. France (3) 3 vs Scotland (8) 21. Parc des Princes.

1 January 1914. France (3) 6 vs Ireland (0) 8. Parc des Princes.

13 April 1914. France (8) 13 vs England (13) 39. Stade Olympique Yves-du-Manoir, Colombes, Paris

**Sergeant Marcel Legrain**
**154ème Régiment d'Infanterie**
**Died 27 June 1915**
**Aged 24**
**Flanker/Number 8**
**Twelve Caps**

*'Pour moi, je n'ai qu'un besoin, celui de réussir.'*
*'I only have one need, that to succeed.'*

Marcel Legrain was born on 14 June 1890 in Paris. A lawyer by profession, he played his club rugby for Stade Français (SF) where he was a forward. He represented France twelve times, the first being against Ireland on 20 March 1909 and the final occasion being against Wales on 2 March 1914. He played for France during their first international victory against Scotland on 2 January 1911 and then against the South African Springboks side in Bordeaux on 11 January 1913 (France didn't play South Africa again for another forty years). He was also one of only a handful of French players to earn more than ten caps.

During the First World War he served as a sergeant with the 154ème Régiment d'Infanterie and was killed in action on 27 June 1915 at Bois de la Guerre on the Marne Sector of the Western Front.

## International Caps

20 March 1909. Ireland (8) 19 vs France (0) 8. Lansdowne Road, Dublin.

28 March 1910. France (3) 3 vs Ireland (8) 8. Parc des Princes.

2 January 1911. France (11) 16 vs Scotland (8) 15. Stade Olympique, Paris.

28 January 1911. England (8) 37 vs France (0) 0. Twickenham.

28 February 1911. France 0 vs Wales 15. Parc des Princes.

25 March 1911. Ireland (0) 25 vs France (5) 5. Mardyke, Cork.

1 January 1913. France (3) 3 vs Scotland (8) 21. Parc des Princes.

11 January 1913. France (5) 5 vs South Africa (11) 38. le Bouscat, Bordeaux.

25 January 1913. England (6) 20 vs France (0) 0. Twickenham.

24 March 1913. Ireland (8) 24 vs France (0) 0. Mardyke, Cork.

1 January 1914. France (3) 6 vs Ireland (0) 8. Parc des Princes.

2 March 1914. Wales (13) 31 vs France (0) 0. St Helen's, Swansea.

**Sergeant Adjudant Alfred (Maysso) Mayssonnié**
**Infantry**
**Died 6 September 1914**
**Aged 30**
**Scrum-half/Fly-Half**
**Three Caps**

*'La justice est le droit du plus faible.'*
*'Justice is the right of the weaker.'*

Alfred (nicknamed Maysso) was born on 10 February 1884 in Toulouse. He played his rugby for Stade Toulousain where his position was scrum-half and fly-half. Toulouse were the champions of France and the Pyrenees in 1912. Mayssonnié was also the strategist of the Red Lady team and played for France three times, the first against England in 1908 and the last against Wales in 1910. He was the only player from the Toulouse team to appear in the first match of the French Five Nations team in 1910.

He was reported missing during the battle of the Marne on 6 September 1914 and later assumed killed on that date.

He is honoured every 11 November, thanks to a *stele* bearing his image affixed to the monument to the dead, Herakles Archer, Toulouse.

## International Caps
1 January 1908. France (0) 0 vs England (6) 19. Stade Olympique, Paris.
2 March 1908. Wales (17) 36. vs France (4) 4. National Stadium, Cardiff.
1 January 1910. Wales (21) 49 vs France (14) 14. St Helen's, Swansea.

**Jean-Sergieant François Poeydebasque**
**249ème Régiment d'Infanterie**
**Died 21 September 1914**
**Aged 23**
**Centre/Fly-Half**
**Two Caps**

*'C'est par la violence que l'on doit établir la liberté.'*
*'It is through violence that one establishes liberty.'*

François Poeydebasque was born on 7 January 1891 in Bayonne. He played his rugby for Rowing Bayonnais at both centre and scrum-half.

During the war he served with the 249ème Régiment d'Infanterie as a sergeant and was killed in action on 21 September 1914 on the Aisne. He is commemorated on the Basque Monument – 249ème Régiment d'Infanterie.

### International Caps
1 January 1914. France (3) 6 vs Ireland (0) 8. Parc des Princes.
2 March 1914. Wales (13) 31 vs France (0) 0. St Helen's, Swansea.

**Captain Robert Balderston Burgess**
**Royal Engineers**
**Died 9 December 1915**
**Aged 24**
**Forward**
**One Cap**

*'Always ready for his duty day and night'*

Robert Balderston Burgess was born on 25 December 1890, the son of Henry and Agnes Burgess of 6R Bickenhall Mansions, Gloucester Place, Portman Square, London, although a native of Kingstown (now Dun Laoghaire), County Dublin. His father was a manager of the LMS Railway Company. While living in County Dublin they resided at Eglinton House, Eglinton Park, Kingstown. Robert was educated at Portora Royal School and Trinity College, Dublin and was said to have been the 'best forward in the invincible Portora team, in whose ranks was the great drop-kicker and punt, R. A. Lloyd. He was honorary secretary of the TCD Rugby Football Club and played for them in all the inter-provincial matches between 1913 and 1914. A fast forward and strong tackler he was never selected again after the record defeat of Ireland by South Africa by four goals and six tries to nil in November 1912, despite the fact that it was generally considered to be the fault of the Irish backs and not its forwards.

As well as his prowess on the rugby field he was also a fine rider to hounds, a first-class shot, and an expert salmon fisherman. After leaving university he was called to the bar, working on the North East circuit and, although successful, had very little time to practise before the outbreak of war. He served in the casualty depot at the North Wall in Dublin during mobilization in 1914 as well as carrying out 'special' work for the French government. He obtained a commission in the Army Service Corps in November 1914 and was rapidly promoted, eventually obtaining a captaincy in the Royal Engineers in January 1915, serving with the Inland Water Transport Unit.

He died on 9 December 1915, at a casualty clearing station after a shell hit him as he was cycling through rue de Dunkerque at Armentières. He was the fourth Irish international to fall in action. His commanding officer wrote of him: 'The late Captain Burgess was an excellent officer, always ready for his duty day and night, and was the most popular officer in his section.'

His name also appears on the war memorial on the entrance to the reading room at Trinity College, Dublin.

Burgess is buried in Bailleul Communal Cemetery Extension Nord (II. B 63).

## International Caps

30 November 1912. Ireland (0) 0 vs South Africa (12) 38. Lansdowne Road, Dublin.

**Captain Ernest Cotton Deane MC**
**Royal Army Medical Corps**
**Died 25 September 1915**
**Aged 28**
**Wing**
**One Cap**

*'Straight, fearless, indefatigable'*

Ernest Cotton Deane was born on 4 May 1887 at Limerick, the third son of Thomas Stanley Deane and Aileen Annie Deane of 27 Cambridge Terrace, York Road, Kingstown, County Dublin. He was educated at Corrig, Kingstown (1901–04), and at the College of Surgeons, passing out with honours (1904–09). While at Corrig he was captain of the rugby XV. He also captained the XV while at Adelaide hospital as well as the Monkstown XV. A superb all round athlete, he won most of his schools cups in a wide range of sports.

In 1909 his international career as a three-quarter was unfortunately cut short when he broke his leg playing against Oxford University in the same year that he had turned out against England in Dublin. By all accounts he had 'a most lovable disposition, he was as modest as he was plucky'.

He was a fine rider to hounds, a great shot, first-class golfer, fisherman and held his own at lawn tennis. He joined the Royal Army Medical Corps in July 1911, training at Millbank and Aldershot. He was sent to India in 1913 and in September 1914, shortly after the outbreak of the war, was sent with the Indian Expeditionary Force to France, landing at Marseilles on the 26th. There he was attached to the 2nd Battalion Leicestershire Regiment in the Meerut Division, Indian Expeditionary Force. As brave on the battlefield as he was on the rugby field he was Mentioned in Despatches twice and awarded the Military Cross. His citation read:

> For conspicuous gallantry on 22nd August, 1915, near Fauquissart. A standing patrol 120 yards in front of our line was bombed by the enemy at about 10 pm, the only notification being two loud bomb explosions. Captain Deane, without any knowledge of the enemy's strength, at once got over the parapet and ran by himself to the spot under rifle and machine-gun fire. Finding four wounded men

he returned for stretchers and got them back into safety. This is not the first time that Captain Deane's gallantry under fire has been brought to notice.

(*London Gazette*, 2 October 1915)

He was killed in action on 25 September 1915, at Neuve Chappelle. An account of the action in which he perished, by Lieutenant George Grossmith, an officer of the battalion, is quoted in Philip Warner's book *The Battle of Loos*.

My battalion, as such, no longer exists; it was decimated, along with nearly all the other regiments of the Meerut Division of our Indian Corps. Of my battalion, there are only two officers and a few men who were not killed or wounded.

His colonel later wrote to his father:

We had a big battle on the 25th and your son went to try and help some wounded in, and was killed, his death being instantaneous … Everyone knew Deane as one of the bravest of the brave, and it was only the other day that he got one of the best deserved and gallantry won honours when he was awarded the Military Cross. I cannot tell you how sorry I am about your son, and how much I sympathize with you and yours in your loss. He was the most gallant fellow I ever met, and we all loved him in the regiment, both officers and men. He was just a part of us, and the few of us left mourn his loss deeply.

He is buried in Rue-du-Bacquerot No 1 Military Cemetery, Laventie, Pas de Calais, France (II. D. 14).

## International Caps
13 February 1909. Ireland (5) 5 vs England (0) 11. Lansdowne Road, Dublin.

Ireland, 1909. Dean standing far left.

**Captain William Victor Edwards**
**7th Bn Royal Dublin Fusiliers**
**Died 29 December 1917**
**Aged 30**
**Forward**
**Two Caps**

*'A splendid specimen of a man'*

William Victor Edwards was born on 16 October 1887, in Strandtown, Belfast, the son of Mrs Mary and the late Mr Alfred Edwards, of The Laurels, Strandtown. His father had been a cabinetmaker and upholsterer with Maguire & Edwards. Educated at Thant College, Margate, Coleraine Academical Institution at Coleraine, County Londonderry. Campbell College, Belmont, Belfast, and Queen's University, Belfast. A member of both Coleraine and Campbell's XVs, he also became a member of the Malone Football Club and Knock Rugby Club, Belfast, which he captained during the years 1911 and 1912, years in which he captained the Malone club as well and played forward for Ulster, appearing for them several times between 1910 and 1912. Edwards finally got his caps for Ireland against England and France in 1912.

On 28 May 1914 he received his final certificate and became a chartered accountant. A strong powerful man he held the 220 yards Irish swimming championship. His strength in the water also led him to represent Ireland several times at water polo.

Having served with the 6th Battalion East Belfast Regiment of the Ulster Volunteer Force, he joined the Army with many fellow members of that body and saw considerable service with 16th (Irish) Division. Edwards was also a prominent founder member of the Active Service Masonic Lodge No. 415 Tipperary, of which he remained a member until his death.

Edwards was commissioned second lieutenant in the 7th (Service) Battalion Royal Dublin Fusiliers on 22 September 1914 in Tipperary. In December he was promoted to lieutenant and in June 1915 to captain before deploying to France with 16th (Irish) Division in February 1916. He became involved in a great deal of fighting and his name appeared twice on the casualty list, once for being gassed and again on 9 September 1916 during the capture of Ginchy when he was wounded on the right side of the head by a machine-gun bullet which left him with a four-inch scar. As a result he was left suffering from dizziness and insomnia for the rest of his life.

Transferring to the regulars with the permanent rank of captain he joined D (set up for Irish rugby players) Company Royal Dublin Fusiliers, 10th (Irish Division), and served with another Irish International, the tragic Jasper Brett.

The division landed at Suvla Bay on the morning of 7 August 1915. The first major battle for the 7th Royal Dublin Fusiliers was the attack on Chocolate Hill on the night of 7/8 August, when they were lent to 31 Brigade. Later, there was protracted fighting on Kizlar Dagh Ridge. The 7th Royal Dublin Fusiliers were taken off the peninsula and brought to Mudros on 29/30 September and landed at Salonika by 24 October 1915.

The 10th (Irish) Division left Macedonia for Egypt in September 1917 and took part in the Third Battle of Gaza between 1 and 7 November. Jerusalem was taken on 9 December and the 10th played a part in its defence for the rest of that month.

Edwards was killed in action near Deir Ibzia, Palestine on 29 December 1917. He was initially buried 700 yards from the south-east corner of the village of Deir Ibzia, ten yards left of the track leading down the hill to the trees. He was then reburied east of the village of Deis Ibsis, close to Mount Horeb at the Jerusalem War Cemetery, Israel (F.26). Amongst his returned possessions were a cigarette case, three devotional books, a (damaged) watch, his whistle and strap, and pipe and pipe lighter.

His name is commemorated on the Strandtown War Memorial, Belfast. His name also appears on a small war memorial near the old Gobbins cliff path on Islandmagee, a peninsula on the east coast of County Antrim, Northern Ireland.

## International Caps
1 January 1912. France (6) 6 vs Ireland (11) 11. Parc des Princes.
10 February 1912. England (3) 15 vs Ireland (0) 0. Twickenham.

**Colonel William Hallaran**
**Royal Army Medical Corps**
**Died 23 January 1917**
**Aged 55**
**Half-Back**
**One Cap**

*'Always put others before himself'*

William Hallaran was born on 19 April 1861. He was the son of the Venerable Thomas Tuckey Hallaran, Archdeacon of Ardfelt and formerly Canon of St Mary's, Limerick. His mother was Lizzie (nee Dawson), the daughter of Richard T. Bunbury Isaac, of Leggagowan, County Down, and of Woodville, County Cork.

William was educated at Dublin University where he read medicine and played several matches for his university. He was selected to play once for Ireland against Wales in 1884. So concerned was he about his father discovering his secret that he played under the pseudonym of R. O. N. Hall. Why his father would have objected to his son representing his country we can only guess.

After qualifying as a doctor he decided to take up a career in the Army and joined the RAMC. He became a surgeon and on 1 March 1915 became a full colonel. During his career he saw much service in Burma, India and Africa. He served in Burma from 1887 to 1889, Chin Lushai, India 1899-1900 and South Africa from 1900 to 1901 where he took part in the relief of Kimberley. He married a local girl by the name of Mary who, after his death, emigrated to America and was last known to be living at 2076, Abington Road, Cleveland, Ohio, USA.

Returning to Jabalpur in India he became Director of Medical Services, dying there on 23 January 1917.

He is commemorated on Face 11 of the Kirkee 1914-1918 Memorial, India.

The Kirkee Memorial commemorates more than 1,800 servicemen who died in India during the First World War, who are buried in civil and cantonment cemeteries in India and Pakistan where their graves can no longer be properly maintained. This total includes the names of 629 servicemen whose remains were brought from Bombay (Sewri) Cemetery for re-interment there in 1960.

His name is on the Sir Patrick Dun's Hospital Great War Memorial, Dublin.

## International Caps
12 April 1884. Wales 1G vs Ireland 0 G. National Stadium, Cardiff.

**Captain Basil Maclear**
**Royal Dublin Fusiliers**
**Died 24 May 1915**
**Aged 34**
**Centre**
**Eleven Caps**

*'A keen soldier, a great athlete, an honest English Gentleman'*

Basil Maclear was born on 7 April 1881 in Portsmouth, England, the fifth son of Major H. W. Maclear (The Buffs) and Mrs Maclear of Bedford and grandson of Sir Thomas Maclear, late Astronomer Royal, Observatory, Cape Town who was also close friends with David Livingstone, as they shared a common interest in the exploration of Africa. The Maclear crater on the Moon is named after him, as is Maclear's Beacon on Table Mountain, the town of Maclear, South Africa and Cape Maclear in Malawi. Two of his brothers were also killed during the war. Lieutenant Colonel Percy Maclear, Royal Dublin Fusiliers, Commanding 2nd Nigeria Regiment, in the Cameroons on 30 August 1914 (commemorated on the Lokoja memorial), and Lieutenant Colonel Harry Maclear DSO near Loos on 16 March 1916 (commemorated in the Mazingarbe Communal Cemetery). His other two brothers fortunately survived the war.

He was educated at Bedford Grammar School where he did exceptionally well and captained the first XV. E. A. Rolfe in the 1929 Old Bedfordians' yearbook wrote of him:

> As a youngster at the Priory School he signalized himself by winning every event in the athletic sports ... At the early age of 15 he played for Blackheath and the records of the time describe him as 'a promising forward, tall, heavy, strong and fast, a resolute tackler and a reliable place-kick.

After leaving school he went to the Royal Military Academy Sandhurst, winning the Sword of Honour. He was gazetted as second lieutenant in the Royal Dublin Fusiliers, served throughout the Boer War, 1899-1902, and was Mentioned in Despatches. He was appointed second in command and adjutant of the Lagos Battalion West African Field Force (WAFF) in 1903, and to the full command 1905.

On returning home he continued with his rugby career. He weighed in at fourteen stone and was just short of six feet in height with a magnificent physique. Described as a forceful rather than subtle player, he was dangerous in attack and formidable in defence, running straight and hard, and handing off with a force, which was only equalled by the tremendous vigour of his tackling. He captained Munster against the All Blacks in 1905. Munster lost thirty-three to nil. He also played for the Officers of the Army vs the Officers of the Royal Navy in February 1907.

Despite Maclear converting ten tries out of twelve at Richmond watched by the England selectors and, despite the fact that they had no place kickers of repute, he still failed to be selected. As a result of being stationed at Fermoy, County Cork, he became eligible to play for Ireland. In his first international he formed part of the Irish team that beat England by the resounding score of seventeen-three Rowland Hill, President of the RFU, commented after seeing him play against England:

> An English soldier stationed in Munster made his debut for Ireland against England at Cork. His name was Basil Maclear and he stamped his authority and class on the match by creating two tries in the first half and scoring another after the interval.

*The Times* was equally praising:

> His defence was very fine, he fitted in well to the passing game . . .displayed a fine turn of speed and . . . was very difficult to stop. Maclear was the key player in the win over Scotland too, and the try he created for Moffatt gave that player his fourth touchdown in three internationals – an Irish record.

In 1911 he was posted to the staff at RMC Sandhurst, where he remained until 25 February 1915 when he went to the Western Front arriving in March. A month later he was dead.

He was killed in action on 24 May 1915, northwest of Wieltje, near Ypres. At about 0300 the Germans launched a heavy gas attack, followed by an infantry assault, which captured trenches from which enfilade fire was directed into the British trenches. The RDF flank was exposed, but they continued to fight. The battalion commander, Lieutenant Colonel A. Lovebrand, was killed. Captain Maclear wetted the gas respirators of the troops near him, and encouraged their defence. In mid-morning Maclear was leading a bombing party to beat back some advancing enemy when he was shot through the throat and killed. After the action, only twenty-one men returned from the trenches, all that remained of the seventeen officers and 651 men who had been 2nd Royal Dublin Fusiliers. Maclear was once again Mentioned in Despatches for his bravery.

Capt Basil Maclear is commemorated on the Ypres (Menin Gate) Memorial, Ieper, West-Vlaanderen, Belgium (Panels 44 and 46).

He was the first Irish International to be killed in the Great War.

## International Caps

11 February 1905. Ireland (6) 17 vs England (0) 3. Mardyke, Cork.

25 February 1905. Scotland (0) 5 vs Ireland (5) 11. Inverleith.

1 March 1905. Wales (10) 10 vs Ireland (3) 3. St Helen's Swansea.

25 November 1905. Ireland (0) vs New Zealand (5) 15. Lansdowne Road, Dublin.

10 February 1906. England (0) 6 vs Ireland (8) 16. Welford Road, Leicester.

24 February 1906. Ireland (0) 6 vs Scotland (10) 13. Lansdowne Road, Dublin.

10 March 1906. Ireland (8) 11 vs Wales (3) 6. Balmoral Showgrounds, Belfast.

24 November 1906. Ireland (3) 12 vs South Africa (12) 15. Balmoral Showgrounds, Belfast.

9 February 1907. Ireland (14) 17 vs England (0) 9. Lansdowne Road, Dublin.

23 February 1907. Scotland (0) 15 vs Ireland (3) 3. Inverleith.

9 March 1907. Wales (6) 29 vs Ireland (0) 0. National Stadium, Cardiff.

**Lieutenant George Herbert McAllan**
**Royal Flying Corps/Royal Air Force**
**South African Medical Corps**
**Died 14 December 1918**
**Aged 40**
**Full Back**
**Two Caps**

*'The first schoolboy to play for Ireland'*

George Herbert McAllan was born on 2 February 1879 in Belfast, the son of Alexander McAllan the manager of the Provincial Bank of Ireland. Educated at Collegiate School, Monaghan and the Royal School Dungannon, he played for Dungannon and in 1896, while still a schoolboy, was selected to play for Ireland against Scotland and then against Scotland; later he also represented Ireland against Wales.

Although he played in the London Irish pre-season warm-up match at Alexander Palace in 1899, he doesn't appear to have been selected for the first XV that season.

In February 1901 he emigrated to Johannesburg, South Africa where he joined the South African Constabulary. He hadn't been in South Africa long when he became involved in the Boer War and was wounded. In 1903 he met and married a local girl by the name of Catherine Hogate.

At the outbreak of the First World War he was gazetted as a second lieutenant in the Royal Flying Corps (February 1915) and was later promoted to lieutenant. After serving with his squadron in England he was posted to German East Africa where he transferred to the South African Medical Corps. He died at Roberts' Heights Hospital, Pretoria, on 14 December 1918 from the effects of injuries received whilst in the Royal Air Force. He was buried in the Thaba Tshwane (old number 1) military cemetery (grave A9) in Gauteng, South Africa.

### International Caps
15 February 1896. Ireland 0 vs Scotland 0. Lansdowne Road, Dublin.
14 March 1896. Ireland 8 vs Wales 4. Lansdowne Road, Dublin.

**Second Lieutenant Vincent McNamara**
**Royal Engineers**
**Died 29 November 1915**
**Aged 24**
**Scrum-half**
**Three Caps**

*'The name of Vincent McNamara will remain the*
*standard of all that is lovely, honourable and good'*

Vincent McNamara was born on 11 April 1891 on Analore, Castle Road, Blackrock, County Cork, the son of Mr Patrick J. and Margaret McNamara. He entered Presentation College, Cork, during the Hilary term in 1902 and in 1904 entered the Christian Brothers' College, Cork, where he remained for seven years, leaving in October 1911 to go up to Cork University to read engineering, being awarded his degree in January 1915. McNamara played in the first XV for both his schools and college, turning out in seventy-two matches for Cork University with only fourteen of those being lost, while forty-four were won and nine drawn. Because of this it is not surprising he caught the eye of the Irish selectors who chose him to represent his country on three occasions. McNamara stood five feet eight inches tall, weighed eleven stone six pounds and was every inch the athlete.

He was commissioned in the Corps of Royal Engineers and posted to 136 Fortress Company which was in 13th Division in VIII Corps. In September 1915, at his own request, he was attached to the mining companies. He had only been serving with them a short time when he met his death on 29 November 1915. After his death his father received the following letter, which told him a little more of his gallant son's fate:

McNamara was in charge of the mining operations on the left section (Fusiliers' Bluff), where connection had been made with the Turkish workings underground. At one point the enemy were forcing lachrymatory gas through to us, and McNamara, at great risk, had successfully mined under them and exploded a charge. He was an officer without a sense of fear and keenly interested in the work, and, unfortunately, went down to investigate without allowing sufficient time for the gasses resulting from our countermine to disperse. He was overcome and despite the most strenuous efforts made by Lieutenant Bernard RE, and several men (all of whom were overcome by the gas in turn) to rescue him, it was impossible to reach him in time to save his life. The loss of this gallant officer was keenly regretted by all the officers and men of the company, and I would like you to convey my sympathy to his relatives.

Yours very truly, H.W. Laws, Major, RE

The letters of condolence came from both his military friends and his civilian ones.

The president of University College, Cork, wrote to Mr Patrick McNamara: 'No more popular and more highly respectable student ever sat on the benches of this college, and it is a real personal grief to me and many others to think we shall not see him again.'

It was left to H.W. Jack, the Irish stand-off, to sum-up Vincent's personality:

'Mackie' was genuine to the core and noted amongst his fellows for his piety. I cannot possibly forget those memorable days of our friendship, when we shared the ups and downs of a football career, in which he always bore the brunt of attack to make my way easy and to make me conspicuous.

Despite being buried on the brow of a hill with his friends standing around him his body was lost and he is commemorated on Lancashire Landing Memorial, Turkey (Panel L.9).

## International Caps
14 February 1914. England (6) 17 vs Ireland (7) 12. Twickenham.
28 February 1914. Ireland (0) 6 vs Scotland (0) 0. Lansdowne Road, Dublin.
14 March 1914. Ireland (3) 3 vs Wales (3) 11. Balmoral Showgrounds, Belfast.

**Major Robertson Stewart Smyth MD**
**Royal Army Medical Corps**
**Died 5 April 1916**
**Aged 36**
**Ireland and Great Britain**
**Forward**
**Six Caps**

*'A fine doctor, a brave soldier, a compassionate man'*

Major Robertson (Robbie) Stewart Smyth was born on 18 August 1879 at 'Seaview' in Warrenpoint, the fourth son of William and Jane Robinson Smyth. He was educated at Dungannon Royal School before going up to Trinity College Dublin to read medicine. After leaving university he became House Surgeon on the resident staff of Sir Patrick Dun's Hospital, Dublin.

Robbie played his rugby for Dublin University's 2nd XV with which he won the Junior League in the 1898/99 season. He became captain of the University XV in 1903/04 before going on to win three caps for Ireland in 1903 and 1904 and three caps for Britain in 1903. A great lover of the game, he also played in three games during the British Lions' tour of South Africa. In addition, he made appearance for both the Barbarians and Wanderers.

Robbie decided to make a career in the Army and was commissioned as a lieutenant in the Royal Army Medical Corps on 31 July 1905. Later, while serving in India (1907-12), he was promoted to captain in 1909.

On the outbreak of war in August 1914 he was posted to France with the British Expeditionary Force. Not only a fine doctor but a first rate soldier, he was Mentioned in Despatches by Field Marshal Sir John French for 'gallant and distinguished service in the field'. He was promoted to major on 2 December 1915. A month later he was gassed and had to be invalided home. On returning to active service he was again gassed in January 1916. This time the gassing was far worse and with Robbie still not fully recovered from the first attack he was sent to a nursing home in London. However, it quickly became clear that his fighting days were over and he relinquished his commission in February of that year. Despite a gallant fight to regain his health he died at 20 Endsleigh Gardens,

London on 5 April 1916, aged thirty-six years. His remains were brought home and buried in Banbridge Municipal Cemetery.

## International Caps

14 February 1903. Ireland (6) 6 vs England (0) 0. Lansdowne Road, Dublin.

28 February 1903. Scotland 3 vs Ireland 0. Inverleith.

26 August 1903. South Africa (10) 10 vs Great Britain (5) 10. Wanderers Ground, Johannesburg.

5 September 1903. South Africa 0 vs Great Britain 0. Athletic Club, Kimberly.

12 September 1903. South Africa 8 vs Great Britain 0. Newlands Stadium, Cape Town.

13 February 1904. England (3) 19 vs Ireland (0) 0. Rectory Field, Blackheath.

**Major Albert Lewis Stewart DSO**
**Royal Irish Rifles**
**Died 4 October 1917**
**Aged 28**
**Centre**
**Three Caps**

*'A most delightful companion … impossible to replace'*

Albert Lewis Stewart was born on 19 February 1889 at Belfast, the son of the late James Stewart (solicitor) and Mrs Stewart of 101 Wellesley Avenue. He was educated at the Royal Belfast Academical Institution (1902-07) and while there he was in the school's first XV (1903-07), the first year as a full back and the following years as a centre three-quarter. He was awarded the school honour cap for the best player, 1905-06, and was vice captain of the team 1906/07. Between 1905 and 1907 he played centre three-quarter in the schools' 'Inter-provincial' Ulster vs Leinster, Ulster winning on every occasion. Stewart was described as:

> the outstanding back of the side. Strong and heavy, and had a useful turn of speed. Takes and gives passes well, and is a fine kicker. Makes lots of opening and can himself go through on occasion. He is equally happy in defence or attack … Can place-kick as is evidenced by the fact that he converted 6 out of 8 tries in the Ulster Schools Cup Semi-final. Knows the game thoroughly.

During the 1906/07 season he kicked twenty-four goals.

He was, as so many Internationals seem to be, a fine all round athlete. Standing six feet two in height and weighing fourteen stone he was in his school cricket 1st XI of 1904 to 1906 and was described as a fine batsman and fielder. An excellent swimmer, he was undefeated in the school relay 'four' in 1905 and 1906. He was in the gymnastic team that won the junior gymnastic competition in 1904 and was also a fine runner, winning several prizes at sprint distances.

After leaving school Stewart joined the North of Ireland Football Club, playing centre three-quarter in the first XV for them between 1907 and 1914. In 1914 all matches were suspended due to the war and their time was given over to drill and preparation with almost every member of the local rugby clubs becoming members of the Ulster

Volunteer Force to resist Home Rule. Stewart was awarded the NIFC Honour Cap in 1908/09 and in 1911/12 he was vice-captain. He represented Ulster on several occasions before finally being selected to play for Ireland, first as a reserve and then against France in 1913. In all he played three times for Ireland and would have received further caps (against England) had he not been a company commander with the UVF and already committed to training with them.

Stewart became a chartered accountant and at the outbreak of the war joined the 10th (South Belfast) Battalion Royal Irish Rifles, which formed part of the 36th (Ulster) Division and was commissioned second lieutenant. They trained at Newcastle, County Down, before moving to Ballykinlar Camp where they remained until May 1915. After that they moved to Seaford, Sussex, and then onto Bramshot. In the spring of 1915 he was promoted to lieutenant and was made the battalion's Machine Gun Officer. On 1 October 1915 Stewart left for France with his battalion. He managed to survive the first day of the Somme, the blackest day in the history of the British Army with almost 60,000 casualties suffered, close to 20,000 of them being killed. Many of his friends and countrymen were not so lucky. During the heavy fighting on the Somme he was recommended for a Victoria Cross (which he never received). He was promoted to captain and appointed to command 22nd Machine Gun Company. In January 1917 he was promoted to major and was again Mentioned in Despatches. In December 1917 it was announced in the *London Gazette* that he been awarded the DSO which, tragically, he did not live to receive.

Stewart was killed in action at Glencorse Wood, Ypres, on 4 October 1917 at the Battle of Broodseinde (Third Ypres), the last successful attack of the Battle of Passchendaele. Using the 'bite and hold' tactic (where the objective was limited to what could be captured and successfully held), the attacking Allied forces conducted an assault on well-entrenched German forces, and showed that it was possible to attack successfully even the stoutest German defences. Albert Stewart was twenty-eight years old and had packed much life into those few years. A fellow officer of the Royal Irish Rifles later wrote to his father:

> I saw him on the night of July 1st 1916 when he came back after being over all day in the German trenches, where he had done such splendid work. He was completely worn out, as he had had a terrible time all day, but he was himself again in the morning of the 2nd.

It was for his actions on this day that he was recommended for the VC.

He is buried in Hooge Crater Cemetery, Ieper, West-Vlaanderen, Belgium (Grave VII, E.14).

## International Caps
8 March 1913. Wales (8) 16 vs Ireland (8) 13. St Helen's, Swansea.
24 March 1913. Ireland (8) 24 vs France (0) 0. Mardyke, Cork.
1 January 1914. France (3) 6 vs Ireland (0) 8. Parc des Princes.

**Captain Alfred Squire Taylor**
**Royal Army Medical Corps**
**Died 31 July 1917**
**Aged 28**
**Centre**
**Four Caps**

*'His death will be mourned by hundreds'*

Alfred Squire Taylor was born on 6 July 1889 in Belfast, the son of the Reverend David A. Taylor DD, of Eastbourne, Windsor Avenue North, Belfast. Educated at Campbell College, Belfast between 1902 and 1907 and at Edinburgh University where he graduated MB BCh in 1914, he won the Honour cap for rugby at school in 1906/07 and at cricket in 1905, also being captain of the XI in 1906. While at Edinburgh University he captained the XV in 1911/12, having played for the university between 1909 and 1911. He played for Ulster and was selected to play for his country on four occasions at centre three-quarter. It was said that, as a player, 'his attack was better than his defence he had plenty of pace and was a fine kicker'.

He was also a fine golfer and played for Malone Golf Club.

He enlisted into the Royal Army Medical Corps in October 1914 and was sent to France in 1915 and then, in 1916, transferred to Mesopotamia. However, he was taken ill and had to be invalided home. After recovering he returned to France in 1917, attached to the Highland Light Infantry in Ypres. He was killed on the first day of The Third Battle of Ypres, 31 July 1917, while dressing the wounds of a fellow officer. A shell fell close to him and killed both Taylor and his patient.

Colonel Pollock of the RAMC wrote of him, 'He was one of the best medical officers, a very gallant officer and a good friend. His death is a great loss to the division.'

The CO of the HLI wrote in a similar vein:

I cannot speak too highly of his work on that morning before he was killed. He had a very keen sense of duty, which he always performed so well. I personally had a great liking for him: he was always cheery under all circumstances.

He is buried in Ypres Town Cemetery Extension (ref III, B 21), Flanders, Belgium and is also commemorated on the Comber Memorial, County Down.

## International Caps
12 February 1910. England (0) 0 vs Ireland (0) 0. Twickenham.
26 February 1910. Ireland (0) vs Scotland (3) 14. Balmoral Showgrounds, Belfast.
12 March 1910. Ireland (3) 3 vs Wales (3) 19. Lansdowne Road, Dublin.
1 January 1912. France (6) 6 vs Ireland (11) 11. Parc des Princes.

# New Zealand

**29720 Private James Alexander Steenson Baird**
**Otago Infantry Regiment, NZEF**
**Died 7 June 1917**
**Aged 23**
**Centre**
**One Cap**

*'Too Young to be an All Black. Too Young to Die'*

James Alexander Steenson Baird was born on 17 December 1893 in Dunedin, the son of James and Lucinda Charlotte Baird. Educated at Caversham School, Zingari Richmond, Otago, where he played centre for his school XV, on leaving school James became a machinist for a local chain company in Andrews Street, Dunedin. In 1913 he made two appearances for Otago. A formidable centre he was also selected to play for the All Blacks for the 1913 test at Carisbrook against Australia, being brought in at the last minute to replace Eric Cockcroft who was injured. The All Blacks won twenty-five-thirteen. It was to be the only time young Baird would play for his country. Despite being selected for the next two tests James was forced withdraw due to a hand injury. More bad luck followed and his 1914 season was ruined due to illness followed by the outbreak of the First World War (It is interesting and tragic to note that six of the All Blacks who played in this 1913 series were killed during the Great War.)

James enlisted into the Otago Infantry Regiment. The regiment was to be involved in some of the bloodiest fighting of the war and picked up the nickname 'The Unlucky Otagos' and suffered more men killed than any other New Zealand Regiment. After his initial training at Tahuna Park, Sports Ground, Dunedin he embarked for Devonport in England, on 16 October 1916, on board HMNZT *66 Willochra*. He arrived with his regiment nine weeks later on 28 December 1916 and after further training was posted to France on 1 February 1917.

On 7 June 1917 his regiment took part in the battle of Messines Ridge in Flanders. The New Zealanders had 3,660 casualties. Of those killed four were 'All Blacks', George Sellars, James McNeece, Reginald Taylor and James Baird. James was seriously wounded at the outset of the battle by artillery fire, being hit in the hands, buttocks and abdomen. He was moved to the 1st Australian Casualty Clearing Station in Bailleul where he died of his wounds; he was only twenty-three years old.

He was buried in the Bailleul Communal Cemetery Extension, Nord, France (III, B.26).

## International Caps
13 September 1913. New Zealand (9) 25 vs Australia (8) 13. Carisbrook, Dunedin.

**9/2048 Corporal Robert (Bobby) Stanley Black**
**Otago Mounted Rifles/2nd Bn Canterbury Rifles**
**Died 21 September 1916**
**Aged 23**
**Fly-Half**
**One Cap**

*'His speed and quick acceleration made him an asset to any club'*

Robert (Bobby) Black was born on 23 August 1893, in Arrowtown, Invercargill, the son of Harry and Emily Black. He later moved to Dunedin where he attended Otago Boys' High and had his first experience of playing competitive rugby. On leaving school he became a bank clerk and began to play for the Dunedin Pirates Club based at Carisbrook Park. In 1911 Bobby made the first of his twelve appearances for Otago. Later he represented South Island and played in their eight-nil victory over North Island in 1914. He also represented the White Star Rugby club in Westport. His speed and quick acceleration made him an asset to any club and he was selected for the All Blacks touring party for their trip to Australia. Bobby played six times for the All Blacks, including the first test where he scored three tries. By the time the team returned from Australia, the Great War had begun and Bobby Black's career was effectively over. He enlisted into the Otago Mounted Rifles and embarked with D Squadron on 4 March 1916 on board HMNZT 47 *Willochra* destined for Egypt. While still on board Bobby was transferred to the Canterbury Infantry Regiment.

Bobby was killed in action during the Battle of the Somme. He went over the top with his regiment on 21 September 1916 to attack the French town of Flers, near Longueval. That day the 1st Canterbury Regiment distinguished itself by capturing a trench at Flers; the cost, however, was high. The regiment suffered 150 men killed against the enemy's 250. Among the New Zealand casualties was the young and talented Robert Black.

He is commemorated on the Caterpillar Valley (New Zealand) Memorial, Somme, France.

**International Caps**
18 July 1914. Australia 0 vs New Zealand 5. Sydney Sports Ground.

**11/448 Sergeant Henry (Norkey) Dewar**
**Machine Gun Section Wellington Mounted Rifles**
**Died 9 August 1915**
**Aged 31**
**Flanker**
**Two Caps**

*'A splendid man in every sense of the word'*

Henry Dewar was born on 13 October 1883, the son of Alexander and Lydia Dewar of 11 Linton Street, Palmerston, North. Norkey, as he came to be known, played number eight for Newton School, Hawera, Star, Stratford, Taranaki, North Island. He was described as a prominent and popular footballer and a splendid man in every sense of the word, straight and strong, and one who commanded the respect of all who knew him. As a footballer he has had few equals in New Zealand at wing forward, where he played a clever 'heady' game.

Henry moved to Taranaki in 1910 and, on leaving school, became an iron moulder working for B. Harkness of Stratford. He played his first provincial rugby with Wellington in 1907. In 1908 he was a member of the Wellington team that beat the Anglo-Welsh touring team but was also a member of the same team that was soundly beaten twenty four-three by Auckland during the Ranfurly Shield Challenge. In 1910 he joined the Taranaki Club side which went on finally to win the Ranfurly Shield. Henry was selected to play in the North Side in the annual inter-island match which took place in 1913. He also played in the Taranaki side that was only narrowly beaten by touring Australians in 1913. His form in all these matches finally won him the converted black shirt of the All Blacks. On 6 September 1913 he played in the thirty-five first test win over the Wallabies at Athletic Park (playing with Norkey that day were Albert Downing and George Sellars who were also killed during the war).

Norkey was then selected for the tour of North America, playing in fourteen of the sixteen games including the fifty one-three thrashing over the All American side to give him his second test cap.

He joined the 9th Wellington East Coast Mounted Rifles as a machine gunner and was based at Awapuni Racecourse, Palmerston North. Probably because he had previously served with the Wellington Naval Artillery Volunteers, Henry was promoted quickly to sergeant. On 16 October 1914, after training, Henry embarked on the *Orari* at Wellington en route for Egypt. After further training in Egypt Henry landed with his regiment on 8 August 1915 at Anzac Cove, Gallipoli. Twenty-four hours later on 9 August 1915, Henry was to lose his life during the epic struggle for Chunuk Bair (Albert Downing, was killed in the same action, being the first All Black to be killed during the Great War).

Of the 8,556 New Zealanders who served during the Gallipoli campaign, 2,721 were killed and 4,742 wounded. Henry is commemorated on the Chunuk Bair (NZ) Memorial, Turkey (Panel 4).

## International Caps

6 September 1913. New Zealand (11) 30 vs Australia (5) 5. Athletic Park, Wellington.

15 November 1913. USA (3) 3 vs New Zealand (27) 51. California Field, Berkeley.

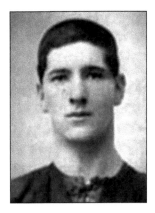

**54336 Lance Sergeant Ernest (Ernie) Henry Dodd**
**2nd Bn 3rd New Zealand Rifle Brigade**
**Died 11 September 1918**
**Aged 38**
**Prop/Hooker**
**One Cap**

*'The bravest of the brave'*

Ernest Henry Dodd was born in Wellington on 21 March 1880, the son of Frederick Henry and Ada Mary Dodd. The family had originally emigrated from Bath in England. Ernie was educated at Wellington College and learned to play rugby under the tutelage of the extraordinary headmaster Joseph Firth, known by all as the Boss. After leaving school Ernie found himself a job as a clerk for the New Zealand Shipping Company based in Wellington. Dodd had tragedy early in his life. In 1904 at the age of twenty-four he married Edith Violet Wills and they had two children Clifford and Lorna. Tragically, Edith died from septicaemia in 1909. A few years later Ernest married again, to Frances Ruby Bolton and they had a son. Sadly, in 1914, she also died, from tuberculosis.

In 1901 Dodd played in the national team's warm-up game against Wellington before appearing in the unofficial international against the touring New South Welshmen. Between 1901 and 1905 Ernie played forty-five times for Wellington as well as playing for the North Island in 1902. He was selected to play in his first and, as it turned out, only international appearance for New Zealand All Blacks in the 'official' test against Australia in September 1905, a match New Zealand won comfortably fourteen-three. Dodd played for the All Blacks a total of three times but this was to be his only international. The word 'official' is used because the original New Zealand team was touring the UK at the time and a second national team had to be created. This match also saw Dodd play alongside Hubert Turtill, another of the All Blacks to die during the war.

On 23 February 1917, although he was thirty-six years old, Ernie enlisted as a rifleman with the New Zealand Rifle Brigade, giving his address as 220a Cuba Street, Wellington. He set sail for Liverpool, England with his regiment on 16 July 1917. Just under a year later, in June 1918, a bullet from a German machine gun creased Dodd's scalp, hospitalizing him for three days. Two months later he contracted scabies and was hospitalized once again. In September 1918 Ernie, together with his regiment, attacked the Trescault Spur, Germany's last line of defence before the infamous Hindenburg Line. His regiment briefly held the ominously named 'Dead Man's Corner' but a fierce German counter-attack drove them out. During this attack, on Wednesday 11 September, Ernie was shot through the throat by a sniper and died from his wounds. He is buried in Metz-en-Couture Communal Cemetery (IV, B.16).

At the end of the war Wellington's headmaster, Joseph Firth, (The Boss), wrote letters of condolence to the families of every one of the 222 old boys of the college who had been killed during the war. On 11 November 1918, Armistice Day. Some time later, Firth was observed standing on the steps overlooking the bottom field where so many rugby matches had taken place with tears running down his face.

### International Caps
2 September 1905. New Zealand (3) 14 vs Australia (3) 3. Tahuna Park, Dunedin.

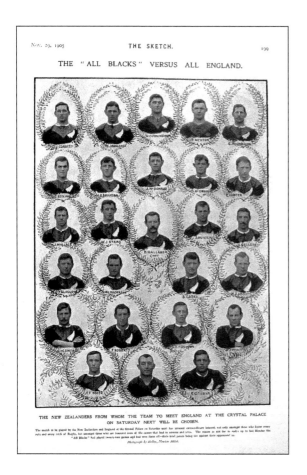

**10/2119 Sergeant Albert (Doolan) Joseph Downing**
**Wellington Regiment NZEF**
**Died 8 August 1915**
**Aged 28**
**Lock**
**Five Caps**

*'The First All Black To Die'*

Albert was born on 12 July 1886 within the bustling Napier port region called 'Port Ahuriri', the son of Mr and Mrs John Downing. He attended the local Ahuriri School in Napier, which was established in 1858 and is still there to this day. Albert first played rugby for Napier Old Boys' Rugby Club, after which he turned out for Marist Brothers Old Boys' Club in Napier. At this time his profession was described as clerk. In 1911 he played in every game during the North Islands Country team five-match tour. North Island Country toured the South Island again in 1912 with Albert appearing in all four tour matches. By 1913 Albert Downing became the first Marist All Black and was part of the successful tour that year, playing in fourteen of the sixteen matches, including the test against All America. He also scored six tries. Tragically, two other All Blacks who played on the tour, Henry Dewar and George Sellars, were also to lose their lives during the war. In 1914 the Marist Brothers Old Boys' Rugby Club had four players in the All Black side which toured Australia. Downing appearing in all three tests and ten of the eleven tour matches, winning high praise for his lineout ability and wonderful pair of hands.

Albert enlisted in 1915. As well as doing his basic training he also played twice for the Trentham Military Forces Team against Wellington and Auckland. Then on 13 June 1915 he left New Zealand with the fifth reinforcements of the Wellington Infantry Battalion heading for Egypt, where they arrived on 24 July 1915.

Albert was killed in action on 8 August 1915 during the attack on Chunuk Bair, Gallipoli. He was the first All Black to be killed during the Great War. The attack on Chunuk Bair began at 9.30 pm on 6 August. After some early successes things began to go hard for the New Zealanders. The following day, 7 August, the Auckland Infantry Battalion attacked and lost 300 men in twenty minutes for a gain of 100 yards. The

Wellington Infantry Battalion was ordered to continue the attack but their commanding officer refused to accept the order, saying he was not willing to allow his men 'to commit suicide'. Early in the morning of the 8th, A Company occupied the Turkish trench on the crest of Chunuk Bair and dug a supporting trench behind it. The Turks' dawn counter-attack saw the British battalions, with the Wellingtons, break and run, but according to a Lance Corporal Hill, it was after Downing had distinguished himself in a bloody bayonet charge. Unfortunately Downing was killed during his heroic attack. He is commemorated on Panel 17 of the Chunuk Bair New Zealand Memorial, Gallipoli.

Twenty-four hours later his friend and fellow All Black Henry Dewar, who had landed in Gallipoli with him, also died in the fighting, making him the second All Black to die in the war.

## International Caps

6 September 1913. New Zealand (11) 30 vs Australia (5) 5. Athletic Park, Wellington.

15 November 1913. USA (3) 3 vs New Zealand (27) 51. California Field, Berkeley.

18 July 1914. Australia (0) 0 vs New Zealand 5. Sydney Sports Ground.

1 August 1914. Australia (0) 0 vs New Zealand (9) 17. Wooloongabba, Brisbane.

15 August 1914. Australia (0) 7 vs New Zealand (3) 22. Sydney Sports Ground.

**32513 Sergeant David Gallaher**
**2nd Bn Auckland Regiment**
**Died 4 October 1917**
**Aged 43**
**New Zealand**
**Wing Forward**
**Six Caps**

*'One of the finest records in the All Blacks history'*

David Gallagher (later Gallaher) was born on 30 October 1873 (he and I share a birthday) at Ramelton, County Donegal, the son of James Henry Gallagher, a shopkeeper. David was the seventh of fourteen children, three of whom died in infancy. In 1878 Gallagher's parents, together with their children, sailed from Belfast on the *Lady Jocelyn* for New Zealand. It was after arriving in New Zealand that the family changed their name from Gallagher to Gallaher to avoid confusion over spelling and pronunciation.

It was at Katikati that David Gallaher first began playing rugby. After his mother lost her job because of illness and his father became too old to work (the family had also had a further four children) Gallaher was forced to leave school aged thirteen and managed to get a job at a local stock and station agent. His mother died of cancer on 9 September 1887 and it was left to the older children to support the family and keep them together. In 1889 the family moved to Auckland and seventeen-year-old David Gallaher got a job at the Northern Roller Mills Company. A good all-round sportsman, he became a member of the junior cricket team recruited from the firm's workers and also began to play junior rugby for the Parnell club. In 1894 the family moved to Freemans Bay. A year later in 1895 David joined the Ponsonby District Rugby Football Club.

On 8 August 1896 Gallaher made his debut for the Auckland provincial rugby side against a touring Queensland team. He was to go on to represent them twenty-six times between 1903 and 1906. In 1897 he was a member of the Auckland team that defeated New Zealand eleven-ten. In the same year he was in the Auckland Championship-winning Ponsonby team.

Gallaher enlisted in the 10th New Zealand Mounted Rifles in January 1901 and took part in the Boer War, remaining in Africa for eighteen months. He served in the Transvaal, Orange Free State and Cape Colony (Cape Province). A natural leader he was promoted to squadron sergeant major. While serving in the war he captained the New Zealand military team that played ten games and won the Army's rugby championship.

Gallaher arrived back in Auckland on 23 August 1902. He was selected for the Auckland team and, on 6 August 1903, played in the initial Ranfurly Shield, which Auckland lost to Wellington six-three.

In 1903, when almost thirty, Gallaher was selected for the New Zealand team which toured Australia that year. He played ten matches – the first five as hooker, and the remainder as wing-forward. He was capped internationally for the first time when New Zealand played its first ever Test match – against Australia in Sydney. In his second international, New Zealand defeated the touring British Isles side at Athletic Park, Wellington, in 1904. A week later he played for Auckland against the tourists and scored one of the tries in their thirteen-nil victory. Gallaher represented New Zealand thirty-six times, playing six tests, and scoring fourteen points (six tries and a single conversion), an outstanding record.

In 1905 Gallaher was named as the tour captain, with Billy Stead as vice-captain. During the tour Gallaher played twenty-six matches, including four of the five tests, and proved to be an outstanding leader and one of the deepest thinkers of the game in his era. The team won thirty-one out of a programme of thirty-two matches and scored 830 points, while their opponents registered only thirty-six points against them. The team's only loss was the historic match against Wales. It was during this 1905 tour of the British Isles that the name All Blacks first occurred. According to team member Billy Wallace, a London newspaper reported that the New Zealand team played as if they were 'all blacks'.

A representative New Zealand team, since referred to as the 'Originals', first toured the British Isles in 1905. This account is more than likely not true. Because of their black playing strip, the side was probably referred to as the *Blacks* before they left New Zealand. Even though the name *All Blacks* probably didn't originate during their trip, the tour certainly popularized it.

He retired after the 1905/06 tour and became a coach and selector (although he did turn out against Marlborough in 1909). He also wrote *The Complete Rugby Footballer* with his friend and fellow player Stead. On 10 October 1906 he married Ellen (Nellie) Ivy May Francis at All Saints' Anglican Church, Ponsonby, Auckland. They had one daughter, Nora.

Although exempt from conscription due to his age, Gallaher still enlisted on 25 July 1916 (taking three years off his age). Because of his service in the Boer War he was promoted to corporal in the 2nd Battalion Auckland Infantry Regiment. He was quickly promoted to sergeant and then company sergeant major. On 16 February 1917 he sailed aboard the *Aparima* heading for Devonport, Plymouth. From there his regiment was sent to France. On 26 June 1917 Gallaher's unit went in action for the first time during the Third Battle for Ypres. His unit then took place in the Third Battle of Ypres (the Passchendaele offensive). On 4 October 1917, during his battalion's attack on Gravenstafel Spur, Gallaher was wounded in the head by a piece of shrapnel that penetrated this helmet. The wound was serious and he died later the same day at No. 3 Australian Casualty Clearing Station, Gravenstafel Spur. He is buried in grave III, D.8 at Nine Elms British Cemetery, Belgium.

## International Caps

15 August 1903. Australia (3) 3 vs (7) 22. Sydney Cricket Ground.

13 August 1904. New Zealand (3) 9 vs 3 (3) Great Britain. Athletic Park, Wellington.

18 November 1905. Scotland (7) 7 vs New Zealand (6) 12. Inverleith.

2 December 1905. England (0) 0 vs New Zealand (9) 15. Crystal Palace.

16 December 1905. Wales (3) 3 vs New Zealand (0) 0. National Stadium, Cardiff.

1 January 1906. France (3) 8 vs New Zealand (18) 38. Parc des Princes.

**35694 Trooper Eric Tristram Harper**
**Canterbury Mounted Rifles**
**Died 30 April 1918**
**Aged 30**
**Centre**
**Two Caps**

*'A fine centre three quarter. Sure with his kicks, a good tackler,*
*plenty of pace, a "Potter" of goals, and a place kick'*

Eric Tristram Harper was born on 1 December 1877 in Christchurch, New Zealand, the son of George and Agnes Harper of 11 Cashel Street, Christchurch. He was educated at St Patrick's College, Wellington from 1889 to 1892 before moving up to the Christchurch Boys' High School. The family was very prominent in New Zealand life with his grandfather having been the first Anglican Bishop of Canterbury. In 1857 Eric's uncle, Leonard Harper, was the first European to cross the Southern Alps. Eric's passion for mountain climbing almost certainly came from Leonard's son, Arthur. Together they made many important discoveries in the Southern Alps and he was also the first to the 6,500-foot Denniston Pass in 1908 and had the distinction of having a creek named after him.

While at St Patrick's College he proved to be a first-class athlete, excelling at sport of all kinds. Eric played for the Christchurch club and then in 1900 for Canterbury. He made fourteen appearances for them up until 1905 and also represented the South Island in both the 1902 and 1905 seasons. In 1904 he made his test debut as a centre half against Great Britain in a one-off international at Athletic Park, Wellington – New Zealand coming out on top nine-three – thus becoming a member of the exclusive 'originals' All Blacks team. Overlooked for the 1905 tour of Australia, he was selected for the touring side for Britain and France. Unfortunately injured early on in the tour, he only played in only four of the first seventeen matches in Britain and in only ten matches overall. He was selected, however, to play against France and impressed by scoring two tries. Eric also picked up the nickname 'Aristocratic Eric' due to the way he stood out (he would always wear black tie for dinner against the rest who were happy with lounge suits) and his social background.

Eric worked for his father's legal firm as a barrister. He was married and had two children and lived at 8 Kilmore Street, West Christchurch. Initially rejected for military service due to varicose veins, after an operation to have them fixed he enlisted in the Canterbury Mounted Rifles. It was then that he discovered that his younger brother, who had already won the DCM and been commissioned, had died of wounds received at Romani in Egypt. Eric embarked for Suez and Egypt on 31 May 1917. After a year of heavy fighting his regiment was detailed to attack the Turkish forward position at Shunet Nimrin, north east of Jerusalem. Eric was killed during this action on 30 April 1918 while under artillery bombardment and attempting to quiet some horses. He was forty years old. He is commemorated on the Jerusalem Memorial, Panel 1, in Israel.

## International Caps
13 August 1904. New Zealand (3) 9 vs Great Britain (3) 3. Athletic Park, Wellington.
1 January 1906. France (3) 8 vs New Zealand (18) 38. Parc des Princes.

**27561 Private James McNeece**
**2nd Bn Otago Infantry Regiment**
**Died 21 June 1917**
**Aged 31**
**Lock**
**Five Caps**

*'A true son of New Zealand'*

James McNeece was born on 24 December 1885, son of James and Edith McNeece of Waikiwi, Invercargill, New Zealand. His parents were Irish-born and he was one of four siblings, three brothers and a sister. James was educated at Middle School Invercargill, Waikiwi, Southland, South Island, where he played flanker. On leaving school he became a farmer. Rugby was his passion from an early age and he played whenever he could (although he was also a fine cricketer representing Southland on many occasions). James played for his local club, Waikiwi. Despite his outstanding all-round talents he was only selected on ten occasions to represent South Island during the 1905 to 1913 seasons in contrast to his brother Alex who played thirty-two times over much of the same period. The brothers played together during Southland's impressive thirteen-eight victory over Australia in 1913, the victory finally gaining James national recognition and inclusion in the All Blacks side which played Australia on 13 and 20 September 1913. The All Blacks won the first test twenty five-thirteen and lost the second five-sixteen. It is only fair to point out here that most of the All Blacks' main players left after the first test for their tour of America, leaving men like McNeece and other Southlander Jimmy Ridland behind. For many years it was considered that there was a prejudice against Southlanders, which resulted in many of their best men failing to be selected to play for the All Blacks.

Even after the All Blacks returned from America, McNeece kept his place in the side and was selected for the All Blacks' tour of Australia. McNeece had a field day. He played in nine matches, scored two tries and appeared in all three tests. It was to be the last time he represented his country.

James joined the 2nd Battalion Otago Infantry Regiment becoming a member of D Company. He embarked from Wellington on 23 September 1916 on board the *Pakeha* destined for Devonport in England. After further training, James finally got to

France at the beginning of 1917 and joined the New Zealand Division at Étaples. His battalion was to be heavily involved in the fighting for Messines, capturing the objective from the Germans who had held it for over two years. Although a great victory it cost some 16,000 casualties to complete. James McNeece was wounded on the morning of the assault, 7 June 1917. Although evacuated from the battlefield to a field hospital he succumbed to his wounds two weeks later on 21 June. James is buried in St Sever Cemetery Extension, Rouen, Seine-Maritime, France (Grave P II, G.3b).

## International Caps

13 September 1913. New Zealand (9) 25 vs Australia (8) 13. Carisbrook, Dunedin.

20 September 1913. New Zealand (5) 5 vs Australia (5) 16. Lancaster Park, Christchurch.

18 July 1914. Australia 0 vs New Zealand 5. Sydney Sports Ground.

1 August 1914. Australia (0) 0 vs New Zealand (9) 17. Wooloongabba, Brisbane.

15 August 1914. Australia (0) 7 vs New Zealand (3) 22. Sydney Sports Ground.

**72271 Rifleman Alexander James Ridland**
**1st Bn 3rd NZ Rifle Brigade, NZ Division**
**Died 5 November 1918**
**Aged 36**
**Prop**
**Three Caps**

*'A versatile forward, he could play in most positions'*

Alexander James (Jimmy) Ridland was born on 3 March 1882 in Invercargill, the son of William Ridland of 13 Dublin Street, North Invercargill. Little seems to be known of his early life other than that he was a blacksmith by profession. He played forward for the Invercargill Star Club, winning several senior titles with them. Between 1906 and 1913 Ridland played in twenty-two matches for Southland, playing against the Anglo-Welsh touring side in 1908, against Auckland in the Ranfurly Shield challenge. He also turned out for the South Island team in 1909, 1910 and 1913. After the 1910 inter-island game he was selected to play in the All Blacks' tour of Australia, playing in six matches including all three tests. One of these tests was to be Australia's first ever win over New Zealand.

It wasn't until 1918 that Ridland enlisted. No one seems sure why he left it so late. After training at Trentham, near Wellington, in 1918, Ridland made the eight-week voyage to England, arriving at 'Sling Camp', Bulford in mid-July. After some further training, he was sent to Étaples in France before joining the highly-respected New Zealand Rifle Brigade who had already seen a lot of fighting. Soon after joining the regiment, Ridland was involved in the fighting at Ancre a la Sambre, at Puisieux au Mont, 'Bloody' Bapaume, Crevecoeur and, finally, Ridland's last battle – le Quesnoy. The little town of le Quesnoy in Northern France had been held by the Germans since August 1914, finally being liberated by the New Zealanders on 4 November 1918. It was to be the division's final action of the First World War. Sadly it was during this action that Jimmy Ridland lost his life, only a week before the end of the war. He had been shot and wounded while trying to storm the town, scaling the walls with thirty-foot ladders (formerly belonging to the French fire brigade). Ninety men of the 12,483 New Zealanders who died on the Western Front died storming the town. Jimmy died of his wounds the following day, 5 November 1918.

So grateful were the people of le Quesnoy for the New Zealanders' sacrifice and their liberation that there are now several streets named after New Zealand. There is also a Place de All Blacks square and a memorial to Lieutenant Leslie Averill, the first officer to go 'over the top' with the Rifle Brigade.

Jimmy Ridland is buried in Caudry British Cemetery, Nord, France (Grave IV, F. 31).

## International Caps

25 June 1910. Australia 0 vs New Zealand 6. Sydney Cricket Ground.

27 June 1910. Australia (3) 11 vs New Zealand (0) 0. Sydney Cricket Ground.

2 July 1910. Australia (5) 13 vs New Zealand (6) 28. Sydney Cricket Ground.

**26923 Private George Maurice Victor Sellars**
**1st Bn Auckland Infantry Regiment, 1 Brigade, NZ**
**Division**
**Died 7 June 1917**
**Aged 31**
**Prop**
**Two Caps**

*'A renowned tough guy, recognized as a hard man in a time*
*when all forwards were expected to have plenty of steel in the ...'*

George Maurice Victor Sellars was born on 16 April 1886, in Auckland, the son of Captain Edward and Henrietta Sellars of 12 Tole Street, Ponsonby, Auckland. He attended the Napier Street School where he played hooker for the school XV. After leaving school he was apprenticed to Mr G. T. Nichol, shipwright, Auckland, in whose employ he remained until he enlisted. George had established himself in the Ponsonby seniors' rugby team as a twenty-year-old in 1906. However, the competition for Auckland places was great and he did not manage to break into the team until 1909. He could not have had a better grounding for his rugby career, a side that had at least five members who had been or were going to be All Blacks. He was also selected to play in the first officially recognized Maori All Black teams in 1910.

Sellars was selected to tour the US in 1913, becoming an All Black for the first time, no national team having been selected since 1910. The All Blacks distinguished themselves throughout the tour, scoring 156 tries with all twenty-three players making it on to the score sheet and even Sellars managing a couple of tries. The All Blacks went on to win all their matches. In all, Sellars played twenty-nine times for his province, as well as playing for North Island in 1912 where he excelled. He was again selected for the New Zealand Maoris in both 1912 and 1914 and played fifteen matches for the All Blacks, including two tests. Although unavailable for the 1914 tour of Australia, he continued to play for Auckland only hanging up his boots when he joined the Army at Trentham Wellington on 30 May 1916.

On 25 September 1916 Sellars boarded the troop ship SS *Devon* bound for Devonport, England. On arrival he was subjected to more training at the NZ 'Sling' Camp in Bulford, finally being posted to France on 1 March 1917. Unfortunately, boys being boys, especially when away from home, he managed to pick up a case of VD from a particularly attractive French girl and was sent to a 'segregation camp' for four weeks. He joined the 1st Battalion Auckland Regiment on 2 June and marched with them to just outside a small undistinguished town by the name of Messines in Belgium. It was here that George was to be killed carrying a wounded comrade to safety on 7 June 1917. He was the first of three All Blacks to lose their lives in a fortnight during the offence and defence of Messines, the other two being Reginald Taylor and Jim McNeece. The same day on which Sellars was killed, another 1913 All Black, James Baird, died of wounds received at Messines. Although Lieutenant McArthur buried George his body was never recovered and his name is commemorated on the Messines Ridge (NZ) Memorial at Mesen, West-Vlaanderen, Belgium.

## International Caps

6 September 1913. New Zealand (11) 30 vs Australia (5) 5. Athletic Park, Wellington.

15 November 1913. USA (3) 3 vs New Zealand (27) 51. California Field, Berkeley

**8/2738 Lance Corporal Reginald Taylor**
**1st Bn Wellington Regiment**
**Died 20 June 1917**
**Aged 28**
**Wing Forward**
**Two Caps**

*'He was a rugby hero in the Taranaki province'*

Reginald Taylor was born on 23 March 1889, in Hillsborough, Taranaki, the son of Thomas Taylor. He spent his early years in and around Inglewood and was a pupil at Inglewood school where he played flanker; his team was Clifton in Waitara. His talents were soon apparent and he went on to represent Taranaki as a wing forward. In 1913 Taylor was selected to play for the All Blacks against the touring Australia side, playing in the last two of the three tests and scoring a try on his debut during the All Blacks' twenty-five to thirteen victory over the Australians. His selection was mainly due to the All Black tour of America, which started after the first test. However, the matches against Australia still carried full cap status and he certainly justified his selection. During his second appearance the All Blacks lost to Australia sixteen-five.

Reginald played for Taranaki against Auckland in the Ranfurly Shield challenges in both 1910 and 1912. Both matches were hard fought with Taylor being on the losing side on both occasions. Then, in 1913, with Taylor playing some of the best rugby of his career, Taranaki finally defeated Auckland, ending the latter's eight-year run of success by beating them fourteen-eleven. Taylor continued in the side representing Taranaki in seven successful defences of the shield in 1914 before finally losing it to Wellington in the last match of the season. He also played for the North Side in the inter-island match the same year, but was not selected for the All Blacks tour of Australia. As with so many rugby careers the outbreak of the First World War brought Taylor's playing days to an end.

Taylor set sail for Egypt where after training he was sent to Gallipoli to take part in the last few months of the campaign before the evacuation. Having survived Gallipoli he was sent to another hellhole, the Somme. After the Somme, Taylor together with his regiment prepared for an assault on a largely unknown little town called Messines which had been held by the Germans since the beginning of the war and was strongly defended. The idea of attacking this armed citadel must have been terrifying even to the bravest of souls. At 3am on 7 June 1917 the Allies commenced their attack by exploding nineteen giant mines which had been laid under the German positions. When they exploded it is estimated that over 10,000 German soldiers were killed and many more left wounded and dazed.

Despite this the fighting was still both fierce and bloody. Even after the New Zealanders captured several important German positions they were subjected to constant shelling and counter-attacks. It was during one of these counter-attacks that Reg Taylor was killed, having managed to survive the battle for two weeks.

Reg Taylor is commemorated at the Underhill Farm Cemetery, Ploegsteert, Comines-Warneton, Belgium (B.6).

## International Caps
13 September 1913. New Zealand (9) 25 vs Australia (8) 13 Carisbrook, Dunedin.
20 September 1913. New Zealand (5) 5 vs Australia (5) 16. Lancaster Park, Christchurch.

**426516 Sergeant Hubert Sydney (Jum) Turtill**
**422 Field Company Royal Engineers**
**KIA 9 April 1918**
**Aged 38**
**New Zealand**
**Full Back**
**One Cap**

*'Considered the finest full back in the world'*

Hubert Turtill was born in Mile End, London on 1 February 1880 but, in 1884, his family moved to New Zealand. Because Hubert was a bit on the plump side he earned the nick name 'Jumbo', which was eventually shortened to 'Jum' a name that was to stay with him for the rest of his life despite his losing weight. He played full back for his Canterbury club, turning out for them eighteen times between 1902 and 1905. Hubert also represented the South Island team in both the 1903 and 1907 seasons. After playing in the combined Canterbury and South Canterbury selection against the touring Australians in 1905, Turtill was included in the New Zealand team for the only international in Dunedin. Even though many of New Zealand's finest players were on their way to England to take part in the 'Originals' tour, New Zealand still managed to defeat Australia fourteen-five, Turtill playing one of the finest games of his career. Despite this, however, it was to be the last time he was selected for the All Blacks.

In 1907 Turtill joined what the Australian papers derogatorily called the 'All Golds' (although in rugby league circles it is considered a badge of honour) or the professional All Blacks for their tour of Great Britain. The team first played in Australia, where they played under rugby league rules winning three matches against New South Wales. The British part of the tour involved thirty-five matches over five months. Turtill played in five internationals in Great Britain and in 1908 had the honour of captaining the side against Australia. At the conclusion of his forty-nine- match, ten-month tour he had taken part in series wins over both Great Britain and Australia and New Zealanders were considered the first world champions of the little known rugby league. It was a historic sporting occasion. However, there was a darker side to the tour. All twenty-eight players who took part, including eight All Blacks, four of them 'Originals' from the 1905/06 tour, were banned from playing rugby union for life. It is also worth

151

pointing out that the tour generated £13,000 for the NZRU, yet many of the players came back penniless and out of work.

On their way home the 'All Golds' stopped off in Australia for a scheduled ten matches, including three tests. Unfortunately, one of the leading lights of the tour, Baskerville, caught pneumonia in Brisbane and died at just twenty-five years of age on 20 May 1907. His body was returned to New Zealand where a benefit match was played in front of a crowd of 8,000 people which raised £300 for Baskerville's mother. This was the first time that a rugby league match was played in New Zealand.

Within two years of this match, eleven former All Blacks were in Great Britain playing professionally. One of these players was Turtill, who returned to England in 1909 together with his wife Mabel and small son Alan and became a popular licensee. He joined St Helen's in Lancashire, making his debut on 2 September 1909 and his final appearance on 21 February 1914. Turtill joined the Royal Engineers and went over to France with his company in 1915 where he was involved in some of the bloodiest battles of the war including the Somme and was lucky to survive through 1916. In 1917 he was moved to the Ypres salient and was involved in further fighting, this time at Pilckem Ridge and Menin Road Ridge. In 1918 Turtill's 55th Division relieved the 42nd Division in the front line at Givenchy and Festubert. It was here on 9 April 1918 that Hubert Turtill was killed by shrapnel from a shell.

After his death his wife moved back to New Zealand with their son. He was also killed in action during the Second World War while serving as a captain in Libya with the 21st Battalion New Zealand Infantry.

Hubert is buried in Brown's Road Military Cemetery, Festubert, Pas de Calais, France (Grave IV, D. 6).

## International Caps
2 September 1905. New Zealand (3) 14 vs Australia (3) 3. Tahuna Park, Dunedin.

# Scotland

**Lieutenant Cecil Halliday Abercrombie**
**Royal Navy**
**(HMS *Defence*)**
**KIA 31 May 1916**
**Aged 29**
**Forward**
**Six Caps**

*'Nothing could have made him miss that fight'*

Lieutenant Cecil Halliday Abercrombie was born at Mozufferpore, India, on 12 September 1886. The son of Walter D. Abercrombie (Indian Police) and Kate E. Abercrombie, he was educated at Allan House, Guildford, Berkhamstead School and Britannia Royal Naval College, Dartmouth. A first class all-round sportsman, he was in the first XI and XV at both schools and at Britannia.

In 1902 he was posted to HMS *Hyacinth* and was one of the brave party under the command of Captain the Hon. Horace Hood, which attacked the Mullah's stronghold at Illig, situated on the east coast of Somalia on 21 April 1904, finally destroying the Mullah's forces once and for all.

An outstanding player between 1910 and 1913 Abercrombie played for Scotland six times. A friend once described his browses on the rugby field:

> Abercrombie's forward play can best be described as that of a dashing player, full of beans ... great speed and height, a good pair of hands, he was, needless to say, a fine touch player ... He was a splendid place kicker, and could place a very long ball, and is credited with some good performances in this important game ... Rugby football is a great and true sport, and it is men like Abercrombie who maintain this tradition.

Abercrombie was also a first class cricketer playing for Hampshire during 1913. At the outbreak of the First World War Abercrombie was on the Mediterranean station but returned home quickly. He was eventually transferred to HMS *Defence* and was with that ship when it sailed out to confront the German Grand Fleet at Jutland.

During the battle of Jutland *Defence* was the flagship of Rear Admiral Sir Robert Arbuthnot, leading the First Cruiser Squadron. During the battle *Defence* was hit by two salvoes from the German ships that caused the aft 9.2-inch magazine to explode. The resulting fire spread via the ammunition passages to the adjacent 7.5-inch magazines, which detonated in turn. The ship exploded at 6.20 with the loss of all men on board (about 903), including Abercrombie.

One of Abercrombie's previous captains later wrote to his wife:

> You and I are in a position to realize to the full the loss that the country has sustained by the death of your husband. I feel perfectly sure that it was his gun that was being fired when the ship gave her final plunge – directly I heard of it, I felt it.

Cecil Halliday Abercrombie is commemorated on the Plymouth Naval Memorial, Panel 10.

## International Caps

26 Feb 1910. Ireland (0) 0 vs Scotland (3) 14. Balmoral Showgrounds, Belfast.

19 March 1910. Scotland (5) 5 vs England (5) 14. Inverleith.

2 January 1911. France (11) 16 vs Scotland (8) 15. Stade Olympique, Paris.

4 February 1911. Scotland (4) 10 vs Wales (7) 32. Inverleith.

1 January 1913. France (3) 3 vs Scotland (8) 21. Parc des Princes.

1 February 1913 Scotland (0) 0 vs Wales (3) 8. Inverleith.

**Captain David McLaren Bain**
**3rd/2nd Bn Gordon Highlanders**
**Died 3 June 1915**
**Aged 24**
**Captain**
**Prop**
**Eleven Caps**

*'Whatso'er thy hand findeth to do, do it with all thy might'*

David McLaren Bain was born in Edinburgh on 10 September 1891, the son of William and Edith Bain, of 42 Moray Place, Edinburgh. He had two brothers, William and George, and a sister, Mary. The family was well off, with the 1901 census showing them having a nurse, a cook, a table maid and two housemaids as part of the household.

He was educated at the Edinburgh Academy Preparatory school between 1897 and 1900 before moving up to the Academy between 1900 and 1910 and Trinity College, Oxford between 1910 and 1914. David played forward for the Academy first XV between 1907 and 1910, captained the XV between 1909 and 1910 and was also in the XI between 1909 and 1910, becoming vice captain in 1910. As if this wasn't enough, he was in the fives team for 1909/10 and captain of fives in 1910 and in the shooting VIII during the same two years.

Bain played for Oxford against Cambridge in 1910, 1911, 1912 and 1913 and was secretary and captain of the Oxford University Rugby Union Club in 1912/13. He not only played for his college, Trinity, at rugby but also at soccer, cricket and golf and had the remarkable honour of being chosen to be the reserve for Scotland against England at Inverleith in 1910 while still at Edinburgh Academy. In March 1911 Bain made the first of eleven appearances for Scotland in the Calcutta Cup match at Twickenham. He played in every game for Scotland for the two years 1912 and 1913, playing against England, Wales and France, South Africa in 1912, Ireland in 1913 and 1914 and Wales in 1914. Bain captained Scotland against Ireland in 1914 but lost his captaincy to F. H. Turner who led Scotland during their next two matches, both of which they lost.

It was said of Bain that he was:

One of those forwards one saw not very much of in the loose, which is generally a good sign, tending to mean that if he is any good at all he is very good. He was certainly a sure tackler, good at the line out, and with an excellent knowledge of the game.

Off the rugby field he was a member of Vincents in 1910, and president 1913/14. On going up, he was also selected as senior commoner of his year and was also a member of the Claret Club and Triflers of Trinity College. When war came he was about to take his examination for the Egyptian Civil Service but joined the Army in August 1914 and was sent to Aberdeen for training where he became assistant adjutant and was placed in charge of musketry. He was eventually sent to France in December 1914 and, the following March, was wounded at Neuve Chapelle. In May he was promoted to captain, returning to the front on the 20th. He was killed by a shell two weeks later while still in his dug-out.

His Commanding Officer wrote to his family, 'He was beloved by all ranks, and his tall commanding figure riding at the head of his men will long be missed.'

Many more officers wrote similar letters noting that David Bain was in every respect a popular man, whose kindly face, lit up by peculiarly pale blue-gray eyes, would long be remembered and mourned. Bain is buried in Brown's Road Military Cemetery, Festubert (VIII, F. 14).

## International Caps

18 March 1911. England (8) 13 vs Scotland (3) 8. Twickenham.

20 January 1912. Scotland (13) 31 vs France (3) 3. Inverleith.

3 February 1912. Wales (7) 21 vs Scotland (3) 6. St Helen's, Swansea.

16 March 1912. Scotland (0) 8 vs England (0) 3. Inverleith.

23 November 1912. Scotland (0) 0 vs South Africa (3) 16. Inverleith.

1 January 1913. France (3) 3 vs Scotland (8) 21. Parc des Princes.

1 February 1913. Scotland (0) 0 vs Wales (3) 8. Inverleith.

22 February 1913. Scotland (18) 29 vs Ireland (5) 14. Inverleith.

15 March 1913. England (3) 3 vs Scotland (0) 0. Twickenham.

7 February 1914. Wales (7) 24 vs Scotland (5) 5. National Stadium, Cardiff.

28 February 1914. Ireland (0) 6 vs Scotland (0) 0. Lansdowne Road, Dublin.

**Surgeon David Revell (Darkie) Bedell-Sivright**
**Royal Navy**
**Died 5 September 1915**
**Aged 34**
**Captain/Forward**
**Twenty-Three Caps**

*'Tis Done, Tis done well'*

David Revell Bedell-Sivright was born at North Cliff, North Queensferry on 8 December 1880, the son of William Henry and Grace Revell Bedell-Sivright. He was educated at Fettes College, Edinburgh where he was in the XV for four years between 1899 and 1902. On leaving school he was accepted at Trinity College, Cambridge to read medicine. At first most people thought the idea of Darkie reading medicine a bit of a joke, but he proved them all wrong by getting first class honours after his first term. While at Cambridge he played rugby for their XV, captaining the side in both 1901 and 1902. Between 1902 and 1903 he also turned out for The Barbarians as well as playing for Fettesian Lorettonian Club (1901), West of Scotland FC and Edinburgh Wanderers. After leaving Cambridge he went back to Scotland to finish his medical training at Edinburgh University, once again playing for the XV and captaining the side. He was one of the few people ever to captain two University XVs, not a bad start to a career and his presence on the field of play stirred memories in all who saw him:

> My earliest recollections of 'Darkie' Sivright are, when I was a small boy at school in Edinburgh, seeing him tearing down the football field, the terror of all school sides ... Cambridge, he very quickly made his mark in the first class Rugby world gaining his blue the first season. He was always a very, very, hard player, and took an absolute delight in the game. To the uninitiated onlooker 'Darkie' appeared to be a rough player, but this was not so ...

On one occasion Darkie stopped the traffic on Princes Street for several hours by lying across the tram tracks. The police knew who he was but wouldn't approach him; they knew his reputation.

Darkie went on to play for Scotland on twenty-two occasions. His first match was against Wales in February 1900 at St Helen's, Swansea. He then had to wait until

February 1901 to gain his second cap, once again against Wales. However, he then went on to play in every match of the seasons 1901, 1902, 1904, 1906, and 1907. In 1903 he played against both Wales and Ireland. During the same year he also toured South Africa with a British Isles team under the captaincy of fellow Scot Mark Morison. At the request of the English Rugby Board he was selected to lead the British Lions on a tour of Australia in 1904 but only turned out once due to a broken leg. He settled there for a year but soon became homesick and returned to Scotland to finish his studies. The next year he played against New Zealand and captained the side (the one and only occasion). In 1908 he once again only played against Wales and Ireland. He also toured in South Africa, Australia, and New Zealand. Darkie's career seemed to break all records and achievements. He was a pioneer of the wing forward role and remains the only Scot to play in three Triple Crown winning sides (1901, 1903 and 1907). He was the only player to tour with the British Isles sides of both 1903 and 1904, captaining the latter tour at the age of twenty-three.

On 25 January 1915, however, Darkie accepted a commission as a surgeon in the Royal Navy. He trained at the Royal Naval Hospital, Hasler, and the Royal Naval Division camp at Blandford. After training in April 1915 he was shipped out with the Hawke Battalion of the Royal Naval Division to the Dardanelles. He wrote to a friend from Gallipoli, 'It makes me swear that I am a medico. I'd be ten times more useful with a parcel of jam-tin bombs and a few Turks in front of me, than a sort of qualified vet.'

While there he was lent out to the Royal Scots Fusiliers (between 8 and 20 June) before being posted on to the Portsmouth Battalion, Royal Marine Light Infantry. It wasn't an enemy bullet or shell that took Darkie's life but, like the poet Rupert Brook, an insect bite and acute septicaemia. He died on 5 September 1915 at the age of thirty-four. A friend recounted his death:

> I have seen a man who was with him nearly to the last. He tells me that Darkie had returned from a long spell in the trenches at an advanced dressing station, and came back properly fagged out. Some sort of insect bit him, and, being in a weak condition, poisoning set in, and he died two days later.

He died on board the hospital ship HMHS *Dunluce Castle*, and was buried at sea off Cape Helles. 'Darkie' is commemorated on the Portsmouth Naval Memorial (Panel MB, BA 7).

## International Caps

27 January 1900. Wales (6) 12 vs Scotland (3) 3. St Helen's, Swansea.

9 February 1901. Scotland (10) 18 vs Wales (0) 8. Inverleith.

23 February 1901. Scotland (9) 9 vs Ireland (5) 5. Inverleith.

9 March 1901. England (0) 3 vs Scotland (15) 18. Rectory Field, Blackheath.

1 February 1902. Wales (14) 14 vs Scotland (5) 5. National Stadium, Cardiff.

22 February 1902. Ireland (0) 5 vs Scotland (0) 0. Balmoral Showgrounds, Belfast.

15 March 1902. Scotland (0) 3 vs England (6) 6. Inverleith.

7 February 1903. Scotland (3) vs Wales (0) 0. Inverleith.

28 February 1903. Scotland (0) vs Ireland (0) 0. Inverleith.

6 February 1904. Wales (13) 21 vs Scotland (0) 3. St Helen's, Swansea.

27 February 1904. Ireland (0) 3 vs Scotland (3) 19. Lansdowne Road, Dublin.

19 March 1904. Scotland (3) 6 vs England (0) 3. Inverleith.

2 July 1904. Australia (0) 0 vs Great Britain (0) 17. Sydney Cricket Ground.

18 November 1905. Scotland (7) 7 vs New Zealand (6) 12. Inverleith.

3 February 1906. Wales (6) 9 vs Scotland (0) 3. National Stadium, Cardiff.

24 February 1906. Ireland (0) 6 vs Scotland (10) 13. Lansdowne Road, Dublin.

17 March 1906. Scotland (3) 3 vs England (3) 9. Inverleith.

17 November 1906. Scotland (0) 6 vs South Africa (0) 0. Hampden Park, Glasgow.

2 February 1907. Scotland (0) 6 vs Wales (3) 3. Inverleith.

23 February 1907. Scotland (0) 15 vs Ireland (3) 3. Inverleith.

16 March 1907. England (0) 3 vs Scotland (0) 8. Rectory Field, Blackheath.

1 February 1908. Wales (3) 6 vs Scotland (5) 5. St Helen's, Swansea.

29 February 1908. Ireland (13) 16 vs Scotland (3) 11. Lansdowne Road, Dublin.

**Second Lieutenant Patrick Charles Bentley Blair**
**5th Bn The Rifle Brigade**
**KIA 6 July 1915**
**Aged 23**
**Prop**
**Five Caps**

*'Truly an outstanding example for future generations'*

Patrick Charles Bentley Blair was born in 1892 at, Wanlockhead, Dumfriesshire, Scotland, son of the Reverend C. Patrick Blair MA, Minister at Wanlockhead for thirty-seven years, and Jean (Jeanie) Bogle Smith.

He was educated at Fettes College, Edinburgh before going up to King's College Cambridge. While at Fettes he played in the XV for three years as well as getting his colours for both hockey and fives. At Oxford he played for both his college and university, taking part in the last four inter-varsity matches before the First World War. He was also captain of the hockey club and played five times for Scotland, against South Africa, Wales, Ireland, England and France.

Blair was a natural athlete, standing six feet in height and weighing thirteen stone. He was also perfectly proportioned, was hard working, first class in a tight scrum and at the line-out. His only real fault was his lack of pace and he was never very conspicuous in the open.

After leaving university he joined the Egyptian Civil Service (Finance Department), quite an accolade in itself as they only took the brightest and the best. Getting a first class degree while at Cambridge probably helped with this (he was one of the few international rugby players who did). However, at the outbreak of the war, he made the decision to leave what was almost certainly going to be a glittering career and return to Britain, arriving home in January 1915. He trained at Cambridge before being commissioned in March 1915 and left for the front during the first week of June. Unfortunately, like so many of his generation, he didn't survive long being killed by a shell at Boesinghe near Ypres while scaling the German parapet at the head of his men during an attack on International Trench.

He is commemorated on Special Memorial IE 10 in Talana Farm Cemetery as, although he is known to have been buried there, his grave could not be located after the war.

## International Caps

23 November 1912. Scotland (0) 0 vs South Africa (3) 16. Inverleith.

1 January 1913. France (3) 3 vs Scotland (8) 21. Parc des Princes.

1 February 1913. Scotland (0) 0 vs Wales (3) 8. Inverleith.

22 February 1913. Scotland (18) 29 vs Ireland (5) 14. Inverleith.

15 March 1913. England (3) 3 vs Scotland (0) 0. Twickenham.

**Lieutenant John Argentine Campbell**
**6th Inniskilling Dragoons**
**Died 1 December 1917**
**Aged 40**
**Forward**
**One Cap**

*'He played the Game'*

John Argentine Campbell was born at Las Flores, Argentina on 20 October 1877. His parents returned him to Scotland for his education and he was at Fettes College for ten years between May 1887 and July 1897 where he played forward for the first XV between 1893 and 1897 and became captain in his last year. As another great all-rounder, he also played cricket, hockey and fives. In the autumn of 1897 Campbell went up to Trinity College, Cambridge and was immediately selected for the university XV, winning his blue playing against Oxford three times at Queen's Club and again became captain in his last year. He also won an athletic blue in 1898 for putting the weight. Campbell went on to play for the West of Scotland before finally being capped for Scotland against Ireland, playing out a draw at Lansdowne Road, Dublin on 24 February 1900. He was considered a hard working forward who tackled hard and was 'vigorous' in all he did.

Campbell was back in Argentina when war was declared in August 1914. He returned home in 1915 and after a brief period of training was sent to France in the spring of 1916 with the 17th Lancers later transferring to the 6th Inniskilling Dragoons.

Campbell was reported missing on 1 December 1917 and little was known about his disappearance. The first news about his fate came from a trooper in his own regiment who, in a letter, told his family how he had carried a badly wounded Lieutenant Campbell to a German dressing station where he left him. In late January 1918 the news the family had been dreading finally came through, unusually from a German officer. He stated in his letter that their son, John Argentine Campbell, had succumbed to his wounds while being cared for at a German dressing station. On hearing the news one of his colleagues wrote, 'Alike at Fettes, at Cambridge, and in the Argentine, his manliness, his straightness, and his modesty won the love and respect of all that came into contact with him ...'

Yet another writing to his father said, 'from the General to the last joined recruit every one admired, respected and loved him, and the colonel said that he was the most magnificent specimen of mankind he had ever come across'.

He is buried in Honnechy British Cemetery (I.A.2). His next of kin was given as Myra G. Campbell.

## Internationals Caps

24 February 1900. Ireland (0) 0 vs Scotland (0) 0. Lansdowne Road, Dublin.

**Captain William Campbell Church**
**1/8th Scottish Rifles**
**Died 29 June 1915**
**Aged 32**
**Wing**
**One Cap**

*'He always had the good of the game at heart'*

William Church was born in 1884 in Glasgow, the son of Major W. R. M. Church (8th Battalion The Cameronians) of 104 West George Street, Glasgow and was educated at the Glasgow Academy between 1893 and 1901, a school in Switzerland in 1902, and Glasgow University from 1904. He played wing three-quarter in the Academy XV in both 1900 and 1902 as well as being a leading member of their gymnastic team. Between 1904 and 1907 he played for Glasgow Academicals and was part of their team that won the Scottish Club Championship in 1904/05. Church also played several times for the famous Inter-City for Glasgow against Edinburgh, and in Scottish Football Union Trials until he got his cap and played in a disastrous match for Scotland at Cardiff in 1906. When the Scottish forwards lost their heads and the match by trying to pick up the loose, though they were undoubtedly the better eight, Wales won by three tries to a penalty goal. William was also selected to play for Scotland against New Zealand but declined the invitation.

William Church was gazetted second lieutenant in the Territorial Force on 5 May 1913 becoming a staff captain on 5 August 1914. He was killed in action in the ill-fated operation in Gallipoli. Church was to meet his end at the head of his men cut down by machine-gun fire within ten yards of the enemy trench.

On hearing of his death his long-time friend Commander J. A. Henry RN commented:

a thorough good fellow, who always played the game. He was a good man to play with or against; and his many games on the wing for Glasgow Academicals, for Glasgow in the inter-city, and for Scotland v Wales brought him many friends. I saw the match at Cardiff, and Billy failed to do himself justice that day. He was quite an unassuming man, who did a lot of good work on the Scottish Rugby Football Union, for he always had the good of the game at heart.

His body was never recovered and he is commemorated on the Helles Memorial, Turkey (Panels 92-97).

## International Caps

3 February 1906. Wales (6) 9 vs Scotland (0) 3. National Stadium.

**Lieutenant Walter Michael Dickson**
**11th Bn Argyll and Sutherland Highlanders**
**Died 26 September 1915**
**Aged 30**
**Full Back**
**Seven Caps**

*'One of the kindest and best of fellows imaginable'*

Walter Michael Dickson was born in South Africa on 23 November 1884 and was educated at Rondebosch College, Cape Town, South Africa, playing full back in their XV. Becoming a Rhodes Scholar he moved up to University College, Oxford and was there at the same time as S. S. L. Steyn, another Rhodes Scholar who won two caps for Scotland and was killed in action on 8 December 1917. (See page 000). In the same Oxford University XV were L. Brown, Australian-born England international, and four other South Africans, K. C. M. Hands, N. Reid, L. R. Broster and W. E. Thomas. Not only did Dickson get his rugby blue at Oxford but he also played for the Blackheath XV and the Barbarians. He quickly came to notice and was selected to play for Scotland, making his test debut against France at Inverleith on 20 January 1912, a game Scotland won by a margin of twenty-eight points. Between 1912 and 1913 he went on to play for Scotland a further six times including against South Africa on 23 November 1912, this time a match they lost by sixteen points. He played his last game for Scotland against Ireland on 22 February 1913. Alongside his many other talents Dickson was also a well-known bulldog breeder and raced motorcars at Brooklands.

One of the stranger sides of Dickson was that he was stone deaf which caused him a few problems in both his private and professional life. During a match against France at the Parc des Princes, Paris, on 1 January 1913, there was something akin to a riot after the game and the referee, Mr A. Baxter, had to thank the great French wing three-quarter Failliot for getting him safely away from the ground in his car. At one point mounted cuirassiers galloped across the pitch to intercept the crowd whose mood was turning increasingly violent. Dickson, quite oblivious of the noise, turned to a brother Scot as the team was making its way off the field and remarked, 'It's awfully sporting of them to take their licking like this, isn't it?'

Dickson was, due mostly to his deafness, a reticent shy man and, although a first-rate player, didn't really shine as did his contemporaries such as S. S. L. Steyn did. However, E. G. Loudon-Shand (Dulwich, Oxford, and Scotland) who had rooms next to Dickson at Oxford said of him, 'he was one of the kindest and best fellows imaginable'.

Dickson was working as a surveyor in South Africa when the First World War broke out. Returning to England quickly, he joined the Argyll and Sutherland Highlanders, travelling with them to France and landing in Boulogne on 9 July 1915. Like so many officers of this time he was killed in action only a few months after arriving, on 26 September 1915.

He is commemorated on the Loos Memorial, Pas de Calais, France (Panels 125 to 127).

## International caps

20 January 1912. Scotland (13) 31 vs France (3) 3. Inverleith.

3 February 1912. Wales (7) 21 vs Scotland (3) 6. St Helens, Swansea.

16 March 1912. Scotland (0) 8 vs England (0) 3. Inverleith.

23 November 1912. Scotland (0) 0 vs South Africa (3) 16. Inverleith.

1 Janruary 1913. France (3) 3 vs Scotland (8) 21. Parc des Princes.

1 February 1913. Scotland (0) 0 vs Wales (3) 8. Inverleith.

22 February 1913. Scotland (18) 29 vs Ireland (5) 14. Inverleith.

**John Dobs**
**Civilian Contractor, Royal Navy**
**Died 30 December 1915**
**Aged 40**
**(HMS *Natal*)**
**Forward**
**Eight Caps**

*'A fine player and fine family man to the end'*

Very little is known about John Dobs who was born on 30 September 1875 in Glasgow and played for Edinburgh Academy and Edinburgh Academicals. An outstanding forward, he went on to play eight times for Scotland between 1895 and 1897.

He worked as a factor for civilian contractors to the Royal Navy. Dobs was friendly with Captain Eric Back, of the Warrior-class destroyer *Natal*, which was at anchor at Cromarty. On 30 December 1915 Captain Back hosted a film party aboard her. He had invited the wives and children of his officers, John Dobs, his wife and three children, and nurses from the nearby hospital ship *Drina* to attend, a total of seven women, one civilian male, and three children. For reasons that have never been properly explained, the *Natal* blew up. The explosion not only killed John Dobs but his wife and three children too. In total, over 404 people were killed when the *Natal* went down, only 299 surviving the explosion. Being a civilian contractor he is not commemorated on any CWGC memorial. However, he is commemorated on Maxton War Memorial in the Borders.

His brother F. P. Dods, 1879-1910, also played for Scotland (one cap).

## International Caps
26 January 1895. Scotland 5 vs Wales 4. Raeburn Place, Edinburgh.

2 March 1895. Scotland 6 vs Ireland 0. Raeburn Place, Edinburgh.

9 March 1895. England (3) 3 vs Scotland (6) 6. Athletic Ground, Richmond.

25 January 1896. Wales 6 vs Scotland 0. National Stadium, Cardiff.

15 February 1896. Ireland 0 vs Scotland 0. Lansdowne Road, Dublin.

14 March 1896. Scotland (3) 11 vs England (0) 0. Old Hampden Park, Glasgow.

20 February 1897. Scotland (3) 8 vs Ireland (0) 3. Powderhall, Edinburgh.

13 March 1897. England 12 vs Scotland 3. Fallow Road, Manchester.

**Major Walter (Wattie) Torrie Forrest MC**
**King's Own Scottish Borderers**
**Died 19 April 1917**
**Aged 37**
**Scotland**
**Full Back**
**Eight Caps**

*'He took risks cheerfully and got out of them*
*by his very daring vivacious style of play'*

Walter Torrie Forrest was born on 14 November 1880 at Kelso, Roxburghshire, the son of George and Margaret Forrest. His father was a famous fishing tackle maker in the town. Educated at Kelso High School, Forrest quickly made an impression as a gifted all-round sportsman. Where he really shone, however, was at rugby, and he became an active member of Hawick Rugby Club, quickly becoming an established member of the Hawick team as a centre.

Walter was first chosen to play for Scotland against Wales in 1903. When news of his 'call up' reached Kelso, a crowd assembled at the station to await his arrival by the last train from Hawick. Forrest became the automatic first choice selection as Scotland's full back. His play, for both the Hawick club and his country, was cavalier, characterized by boundless energy and vigour with an apparent disregard for his own safety. A contemporary commented, 'Forrest gets into these 'hats' for the sake of getting out of 'em!'

Forrest went on to play in every International match for Scotland for the season 1903/04 and again in 1905 against Ireland and Wales. It is certainly worth noting that, in both 1903 and 1904, Scotland were the International Champions. However, due to a broken collarbone, sustained while playing for Hawick two days before, he missed the 1905 Calcutta Cup match at Richmond. Although the injury ended his International career he continued to play three-quarter for Kelso.

Forrest was a Territorial Force officer before the war with the King's Own Scottish Borderers. He was posted to the 4th Battalion and sent to Gallipoli where he was lucky to survive the appalling casualties taken by the battalion. From Gallipoli the battalion was sent to Palestine where they were to suffer further and heavy losses. Forrest was not only promoted to major but also went on to earn the Military Cross:

Major, 1/4th Battalion, King's Own Scottish Borderers, 155th (South Scottish) Brigade, 52nd (Lowland) Division; Mentioned in Despatches and MC, Gazetted 25 November 1916:

For conspicuous gallantry in action. He carried out a daring reconnaissance and obtained most valuable information. He has on many previous occasions done very fine work.

On 19 April 1917, during the second battle of Gaza, 1/4 KOSB, which had been held in reserve, were ordered forward to retake the Turkish redoubt positioned on Outpost Hill. The following is an account of the action on that day:

The officer in command of the attack, Major Walter Forrest, rallied the remaining survivors of the previous attacks and together with his own men, gave the order to fix bayonets and await the command to charge. An observer later wrote: 'When all was ready, Major Forrest, the Wattie Forrest of the football field, led his men forward for the last time. This charge of men from almost every unit in the 155th Brigade was a most inspiring sight. Under a murderous fire, which struck down many, they rushed up the hill. Major Forrest was mortally wounded as he entered the work, and there fell one of the best of soldiers, best of friends and best of sportsmen in the Division.

Major Forrest is buried in Gaza War Cemetery, Israel (VII, C. 9).

Forrest was a close friend of the war poet Wilfred Owen who was badly affected by his death.

## International Caps

7 February 1903. Scotland (3) 6 vs Wales (0) 0. Inverleith.

28 February 1903. Scotland (0) 3 vs Ireland (0) 0. Inverleith.

21 March 1903. England (3) 6 vs Scotland (7) 10. Athletic Ground, Richmond.

6 February 1904. Wales (13) 21 vs Scotland (0) 3. St Helen's, Swansea.

27 February 1904. Ireland (0) 3 vs Scotland (3) 19. Lansdowne Road, Dublin.

19 March 1904. Scotland (3) 6 vs England (0) 3. Inverleith.

4 February 1905. Scotland (3) 3 vs Wales (3) 6. Inverleith.

25 February 1905. Scotland (0) 5 vs Ireland (5) 11. Inverleith.

**Captain Rowland Fraser**
**1st Bn The Rifle Brigade**
**Died 1 July 1916**
**Aged 26**
**Prop**
**Four Caps**

*'The heart of the entire rugby football world bows in*
*respectful sympathy before such sorrow'*

Roland Fraser was born on 10 January 1890, the son of J. M. Fraser, of Invermay, Forgandenny and educated at the Merchiston Preparatory (1900-03) followed by Merchiston Castle School Edinburgh (1903-08) and then Pembroke College Cambridge (1908-11). He was in the Merchiston Castle School XV between 1905 and 1908 as well as being in the XI for the same years, captaining the side in 1908. While at Cambridge he played for the XV against Oxford (1908-10) and was captain in 1910. He was never on the winning side, although Cambridge made a draw against Oxford in 1908 with one goal each.

He went on to play for Scotland on four occasions in 1911 but, once again, never on the winning side, this being the only year France won an international match. It must be quite unusual for a player to be a University blue, and an international player and yet never be on the winning side. It was of course in no way Rowland's fault that he held this unenviable record. He was a first-class forward, hardworking, risk taking, a wonderful tackler and solid handler. After going down he played for Edinburgh University.

Fraser received a commission in the Rifle Brigade on 5 August 1914 and was sent to train in Sheerness with the 6th Battalion. Crossing to France with his regiment on 4 January 1915, he quickly came to notice and was promoted to lieutenant in August 1915. The following November he became a captain and between July and November 1915 was the battalion's machine-gun officer. It's worth noting that in his division in France there were twenty-seven rugby internationals all of whom he had played against at some time or the other. In April 1915 he played in a game for 4th Division against a freshly arrived South Midlands Division. This time he was on the winning side. In June 1916 he was granted leave to marry and on the 20th of that month married Miss May Dorothy Ross of Invinidi, USA, returning to France the following day.

A few weeks after his return he was to take place in the biggest offensive of the First World War to that time, which began on 1 July 1916, the first day of the Somme. On this day the British Army suffered more casualties than it had in any other day in its history to that date. The British Army was to suffer over 60,000 casualties, 20,000 of whom were to lose their lives. One of those casualties was to be Captain Rowland Fraser. A letter sent home to his wife explained the circumstances of his death:

He was leading his company in an attack when he was shot in the side by a machine-gun bullet, within a few yards of the German trenches. His orderly got him into a shell-hole and dressed his wound, but he was again hit in the side by shrapnel. He only lived for six hours, his orderly staying with him till the end.

A letter from his orderly outlined his personal experiences, 'Captain Frazer was one of the bravest men that ever lived, and he died like the Officer and gentleman that he was.'

Rowland is commemorated on the Thiepval Memorial (Pier and face 16B and 16C).

## International Caps

2 January 1911. France (11) 16 vs Scotland (8) 15. Stade Olympique Yves-dumanoir, Colombes, Paris.

4 February 1911. Scotland (4) 10 vs Wales (7) 32. Inverleith.

25 February 1911. Scotland (3) 10 vs Ireland (8) 16. Inverleith.

18 March 1911. England (8) 12 vs Scotland (3) 8 Twickenham.

**Major Roland Elphinstone Gordon MC**
**C Battery 251st Brigade, Royal Field Artillery**
**Died 30 August 1918**
**Aged 25**
**Centre**
**Three Caps**

*'He was, indeed, one to be envied – his happy disposition,*
*his peerless ability at our great game, and his glorious death'*

Roland Elphinstone Gordon was born at Selangor, Straits Settlements, Malaya, on 22 January 1893, the son of George Dalrymple Gordon, of the Government Irrigation Department, Ceylon and Georgina Meredith of 'Alwyns', Teignmouth, South Devon. He was educated at the King's School, Canterbury and played for the first XV at right three-quarter between 1909 and 1911, as well as being a member of the five pairs between the same dates.

In 1911 he entered the Royal Military Academy, Woolwich coming forty-fifth in the entry exam. While at Woolwich he became captain of the rugby XV and also represented the Royal Artillery and the Army. On 22 January 1913 he was commissioned as a second lieutenant in the Royal Artillery. It wasn't long before Scotland saw his worth and he went on to play for them on three occasions. He played brilliantly against France at the Parc des Princes on 1 January 1913 and scored two, contributing greatly towards Scotland's twenty one-three victory before going on to play against Wales at Inverleith on 1 February 1913, Wales winning this time eight-nil. His final match was against Ireland, again at Inverleith; this time Scotland emerged as victors twenty nine-fourteen.

His international career was cut short when he was posted to India in late 1913 attached to 82 Battery Royal Field Artillery (RFA), stationed at Kirki. In November 1914, shortly after the outbreak of the First World War, he was posted to Mesopotamia where he was seriously wounded in action during the summer of 1915 and returned home. Not that he was about to let serious wounds stop him playing: while convalescing he not only coached the RA cadets at Exeter but also played for the Cadet XV during the 1916/17 season. Before returning to the front he played one more big game, this time against the previously undefeated Army Service Corps XV at Rectory Field, Blackheath.

It was mainly due to his great performance at the centre that the ASC were beaten, his winning try in the last minute of the match proving decisive.

He recovered well and returned to the front in 1917, this time to France. He was wounded again in June of that year and again for a third time in May 1918. He was also awarded an MC in the King's Birthday Honours of June 1918 (*London Gazette*, 3 June 1918) and was also Mentioned in Despatches. In August 1918 he was wounded for a fourth and final time, this time succumbing to his wounds. Not even this brave heart could stop his inevitable fate.

He is buried in the Daours Communal Cemetery (Extension VIII, B. 3), Somme, France.

## International Caps

1 January 1913. France (3) 3 vs Scotland (8) 21. Parc des Princes.
1 February 1913. Scotland (0) 0 vs Wales (3) 8. Inverleith.
22 February 1913. Scotland (18) 29 vs Ireland (5) 14. Inverleith.

**Lieutenant James Young (JY) Milne Henderson**
**11th Bn Highland Light Infantry**
**Died 31 July 1917**
**Aged 26**
**Fly-Half**
**One Cap**

*'Perhaps no man who has played in but one International*
*game will be so long and so well remembered as he was ...'*

James Young Milne Henderson was born in Edinburgh on 9 March 1891, the son of John and Ina Milne-Henderson of 15 Merchiston Park. Educated at George Watson's College, where at the tender age of thirteen he was already in the second XV, getting into the first XV two years later at the age of fifteen, he was seen by many as the best stand-off ever to come out of Watson College. Like so many international players he also excelled in several other sports and was a fine cricketer, hockey player and swimmer (East of Scotland Swimming Champion).

He only played for Scotland once against England before business commitments took him to Travancore, South India, in 1911. While in India he didn't let his keen interest in the sport wane and played for Madras.

Returning to England he became works manager for Messrs McVitie and Price, Willesden, London. At the outbreak of war he was commissioned in the Highland Light Infantry. Like so many other internationals he wasn't destined to survive the war. On 31 July 1917, during the opening day of the Third Battle of Ypres, the 11th Highland Light Infantry (HLI) attacked enemy positions situated at Square Farm, Hill 35 and Frost House. The Highland Light Infantry took Low Farm, but were checked by fire from Pommern Castle and Hill 35. Lieutenant Henderson was killed during this action.

He is commemorated on the Ypres (Menin Gate) Memorial, Ieper, West-Vlaanderen, Belgium (Panel 38).

On learning of his death an unknown fellow officer commented:

When 'J.Y.' fell in the forefront of battle a splendid young Scot was taken from us, and the game of Rugby football was robbed of an ornament. Perhaps no man who has played in but one International game will be so well and so long remembered as he will, and in that fact rests a great tribute to the man himself apart from his personal prowess on the football field.

The character of the man can perhaps best be illustrated through his last letter home dated 26 July 1917: 'If I have to go, I will be quite happy, as I will go doing my duty.'

Captain A. S. Taylor, an Irish international, who was a Royal Army Medical Corps doctor attached to the Highland Light Infantry, was killed in action on the same day. His brother was killed with the Royal Flying Corps some time later.

## International Caps
18 March 1911. England (8) 13 vs Scotland (3) 8. Twickenham.

**Lieutenant David Dickie Howie**
**Royal Field Artillery**
**Died 19 January 1916**
**Aged 27**
**Lock**
**Seven Caps**

*'A most popular man'*

David Dickie Howie was born on 12 May 1889 at Rosebery Temple, Midlothian, the son of Archibald and Jessie Howie (formerly Mitchell) of The Grange, Kinghorn, Fife. He was educated at Kirkcaldy High School where he was a forward on the school XV for three years and won the Nairn Cup for the champion athlete at the school in 1903. In 1912 he played forward for Scotland against Wales, Ireland, England, France and South Africa and the next year was capped again, this time against Wales and France, earning seven caps in all.

Before the war Howie was a farmer. He married Marie Winifred Gibson and they lived at 1 Mayfield Gardens, Edinburgh. They had one child, Eleanor Margot Linton Dickie, who was born at Skegness on 4 May 1915.

On 2 September 1914, shortly after the outbreak of the war, he enlisted as a trooper (regimental number 2033) in the Fife and Forfar Yeomanry at Kirkcaldy. He trained in England until he was commissioned as a second lieutenant in the City of Glasgow Battery, Highland Brigade, Royal Field Artillery.

Howie embarked with his battery at Devonport on 18 August 1915 and landed at Alexandria on 1 September 1915. He was posted to 1/5 Battery, 1/4th Lowland (Howitzer) Brigade, RFA in Gallipoli. On 28 September 1915 he was admitted to the 13th Casualty Clearing Station and released for duty on 4 October 1915.

During the evacuation of Gallipoli he caught a chill and, on 16 January 1916, was admitted to the Anglo-American Hospital in Cairo suffering from pneumonia. He died on 19 January 1916 of 'self-inflicted revolver wounds, whilst temporarily of unsound mind, due to the delirium of pneumonia'.

A Court of Enquiry was held in Cairo on 3 February 1916. One of the witnesses, Nursing Sister Laycock, AS QAIMNSR, stated that she:

was on duty when Lieutenant Howie entered the Hospital. He was very ill but fairly quiet. He was suffering from delusions and slightly delirious. On the 17th January he was much worse and became worse on the 18th. I took the report for the night of the 18th at 8 o'clock on the morning of the 19th. He was reported to be much better. The patient was quiet and drowsy most of the day. He took his nourishment well, and when I last saw him about five minutes before his death he was apparently sleeping. As I entered the room again I heard the revolver report, and saw the patient still in the position he would be in, in shooting himself …

He was buried in the British Cemetery, Old Cairo (Grave No. 267 D).

His brother Robert Howie won four caps for Scotland in 1924.

## International Caps

20 January 1912. Scotland (13) 31 vs France (3) 3. Inverleith.

3 February 1912, Wales (7) 21 vs Scotland (3) 6. St Helen's, Swansea.

24 February 1912. Ireland (7) 10 vs Scotland (3) 8. Lansdowne Road, Dublin.

16 March 1912. Scotland (0) 8 vs England (0) 3. Inverleith.

23 November 1912. Scotland (0) 0 vs South Africa (3) 16. Inverleith.

1 January 1913. France (3) 3 vs Scotland (8) 21. Parc des Princes.

1 February 1913. Scotland (0) 0 vs Wales (3) 8. Inverleith.

**Lieutenant James Laidlaw Huggan**
**Royal Army Medical Corps, attd 3rd Bn**
**Coldstream Guards**
**KIA 16 September 1914**
**Aged 25**
**Wing**
**One Cap**

*'If ever I met a brave man, he was'*

James Laidlaw Huggan was born in Jedburgh, Roxburghshire, on 11 October 1888, the son of Robert Huggan, an engineer. Huggan learned to play rugby with the Jed Forest team, the club of his native town with whom he played wing three-quarter for several seasons. He was first educated at Watson's college Edinburgh before moving onto Queen Elizabeth Grammar School, Darlington where he was captain of the school football and cricket between 1905 and 1906. At Edinburgh University he read medicine and while studying also played wing three-quarter for the university XI, as well as representing the university at association football and winning a blue for athletics, a rare achievement. After graduating with first-class honours in surgery, he became house surgeon to Mr Alexander Miles, surgeon to the Edinburgh Royal Infirmary, who later described him as one of the finest young men he had ever met.

Huggan went on to play for London Scottish as well as for the Army against the Navy. It was during one of these games that his ability was noticed which led the selectors to choose him to play for Scotland against England in 1914. His forte was:

> an all-out dash and energy, hard for the line, as hard as he could go. This lent to his game a character for sheer 'bullocking' which, I believe told against him, but which was unmerited … but it was in carrying out the chief duty of a wing, which is to score tries, that Huggan shone.

He scored one of the Scottish tries and gave such an impressive demonstration that he was thought by all to be one of the best three-quarters in the game.

Huggan was gazetted to the RAMC in 1912. He was about to leave for India in 1914 when war broke out and he was attached to the 3rd Battalion Coldstream Guards, sailing for France with them on 13 August 1914. After numerous acts of bravery leading to his recommendation for the Victoria Cross, he was eventually killed in action on 16 September 1914. The following letter was sent by Huggan's commanding officer, Lieutenant Colonel G. Fielding to his brother:

> If ever I met a brave man, he was. At Landrecies, when under heavy fire for some hours during the night, he remained up in the front all night, helping and dressing the wounded as coolly as if he was in a hospital in time of peace. At Villers-Cotterêts he was conspicuous for his bravery. This was a rearguard action, and the line was being gradually pushed back; but he was always in the rear, and sometimes even nearer to the enemy, dressing the wounded and helping them back. At the Aisne he was most conspicuous everywhere. On the day on which he was killed he again did a very brave action. There were in a barn about sixty wounded Germans; they were all cases that could not move without help. The Germans shelled this barn and set it on fire. Your brother, in spite of shot and shell raining about him, called for volunteers to help him save these wounded men from the burning building, and I am glad to say it was greatly in consequence of his bravery that they were all saved. After he had run this great danger successfully, he moved many of his wounded men to a quarry in rear, when a big shell came into it and killed him and many others. He was buried near where he fell, in the garden of la Cour de Soupir Farm. The whole battalion regretted his loss, as we had all got very fond of him, and admired him as a really brave man, always ready to sacrifice himself for the good of those who should happen to come under him for treatment.

The remarkable thing about this letter is that it shows that Huggan died saving the lives of sixty German wounded and not British. It might also explain why the recommendation for the VC was not carried forward. However, if nothing else, it shows the great compassion of the man and the serious way in which he took his Hippocratic Oath. In the end, Huggan was Mentioned in Sir John French's Despatches of 8 October 1914 for this and several other brave actions.

He is commemorated on the la Ferte-Sous-Jouarre Memorial to the missing in France.

## International Caps
21 March 1914. Scotland (3) 15 vs England (3) 16. Inverleith.

**Captain William Ramsay Hutchison**
**6/7th Royal Scots Fusiliers**
**Died 22 March 1918**
**Aged 29**
**Lock**
**One Cap**

*'Multis Ille Bonis Flebilis Occidit'*

William Ramsay Hutchison was born on 16 January 1889, the son of John Hutchison MA LLD and Mrs Margaret Paterson McCall Hutchison of 4 St John's Terrace, Hillhead, Glasgow. He was educated at the Glasgow High School and, before leaving in 1905, had not only represented their first XV but also captained the side. After leaving school he played for his 'old boys' team (1905-11), once again captaining the side in 1908/09.

When Hutchison first began to play the 'Great Game' he played as a half back, but after 1909 changed his position to forward. In 1911 he not only represented Glasgow in the inter-city match with Edinburgh, but was also selected to play for Scotland against England. He was a hard-working forward, whose long experience of play outside the scrummage was invaluable to him in big matches. Although Scotland lost the match, the reason for the defeat cannot be laid at Hutchison's door. There is no doubt that this would not have been his only cap had he not decided to further his career in Canada.

When the war broke out Hutchison was on holiday in Scotland and in September 1914 joined the ranks of the 17th Battalion Highland Light Infantry. After a brief period of training he was commissioned in the Royal Scots Fusiliers. He went first went to France before being sent to Salonika but was invalided home after being seriously wounded. After he recovered, he returned to France, being stationed at Arras.

He was killed in action during the fighting on the second day of the Germans' Ludendorff offensive on 22 March 1918. A brother officer wrote of the circumstances:

> He was my company commander, and the two of us were together during the first two days of the great German push. A critical moment had been reached on the afternoon of the second day. With one half of the company I started to dig a line of defence, while Captain Hutchison, with the other half, went forward on my right to form a strong post. Machine-gun fire was intense and he was hit when he had gone forward about a quarter of an hour.

182

He is commemorated on the Arras Memorial, Pas de Calais, France (Bay 5).

'Multis ille bonis flebilis occidit'

(His death is to be lamented by many worthy people)

## International Caps

18 March 1911. England (8) 13 vs Scotland (3) 8. Twickenham.

**Lieutenant Colonel George Alexander Walker Lamond**
**Royal Engineers**
**Died 25 February 1918**
**Aged 39**
**Centre**
**Three Caps**

*'He helped build an empire'*

George Lamond was born in Glasgow on 23 July 1878, the son of Robert and Isabella Lomond and educated at the Kelvinside Academy. Although only sixteen years of age, he was given a place as a three-quarter in the Kelvinside Academicals XV. He went on to play centre in the inter-city and in the City's team against the rest of Scotland in 1896, wing in these fixtures in 1897, and again centre for Glasgow in the Inter-City of 1898. In 1899 he received his first cap for Scotland against Wales. During the match he dropped the goal that put Scotland into the lead and eventually led to their victory. He played against England in the same year but was lost to Scotland after that, having to develop his career in Egypt.

After leaving school he trained as a civil engineer in the offices of Messrs Formans and McCall, CE. After serving his apprenticeship he found work with Sir John Aird, public works contractors, working in both the UK and Egypt, where he was involved in the construction of the three famous Nile barrages at Esnah, Assiut and Assuan. As a result of his work he was decorated with the Orders of the Medjidieh and Osmanieh by the Egyptian and Turkish Governments. Somewhere within his hectic life he found time to marry his girlfriend, Jean Caven Leishman.

Returning to England in 1902, he was employed in the construction of Royal Edward Dock at Avonmouth. He continued to play rugby and represented Bristol City for three years, becoming their captain in his final season. During this time he also turned out for the Gloucestershire County team. In 1905 he won his third cap for Scotland and was in the team that defeated England at Richmond. Returning to Egypt with his work, Lamond finally retired from rugby although he remained a keen golfer, playing off scratch, tennis player and, when he got the chance, fly fisherman.

At the outbreak of the Great War, Lamond returned home and, after being employed on government work on Salisbury Plain, was given a commission in the Royal Engineers. Being deployed to France he was soon engaged in numerous engineering projects and heavy fighting. As a result he received rapid promotion, becoming a lieutenant colonel. In 1917 he was sent to Mesopotamia and given a job on the staff where he was in charge of the construction and organization of the new port and works on the Twin Rivers. As a result of the work he was mentioned in Sir Stanley Maude's Despatches. Unfortunately, like so many soldiers serving in that country, he succumbed to a fever and was invalided to Colombo in Ceylon (now Sri Lanka). However, it made very little difference and on 25 February 1918 he died.

He is buried in the Colombo (Kanatte) General Cemetery (Pres. V, CC.21).

He is also commemorated on the golf club memorial at Elie in Fife.

## International Caps

4 March 1899. Scotland (3) 21 vs Wales (10) 10. Inverleith.

11 March 1899. England (0) 0 vs Scotland (0) 5. Rectory Field, Blackheath.

18 March 1905. England (0) 0 vs Scotland (0) 8. Athletic Ground, Richmond.

**Lieutenant Eric (Puss) Milroy**
**8th Bn The Black Watch (Royal Highland**
**Regiment)**
**Died 18 July 1916**
**Aged 28**
**Captain**
**Scrum-half**
**Twelve Caps**

*'With Sudden brightness, like a man inspired'*

Eric (Puss) Milroy was born in Edinburgh on 4 December 1887, the second son of Alexander MacLeod Milroy, a bank agent, and Margaret Walteria Milroy of 16 Abbotsford Park, Edinburgh. He had one brother, Alexander, and two sisters, Margaret and Jessie, and was educated, like so many of his contemporaries, at George Watson's College between 1894 and 1906, where he was in the school XV as a scrum-half in 1905/06 and gained the Watsonian Medal for combined scholarship and athletics. Milroy also served as a sergeant in the cadet corps. After leaving school he went up to Edinburgh University to read mathematics, having won an open bursary, and gained an MA with honours. Milroy didn't play for his university, choosing instead to play for his school's former pupils club, the 'Watsonians', at scrum-half once again.

Between 1910 and 1914 Milroy played twelve times for Scotland including the infamous 'riot' match at the Parc des Princes in Paris in 1913. He also went to South Africa with Dr R. S. Smyth's team in 1910 but, due to illness, only played three times. For many years Milroy was overlooked as an international, the SRU not thinking him good enough for the XV. How wrong they were. After playing for Scotland eleven times in March 1914 he was selected as captain for their last international match before the war. The game was played at Inverleith and is considered to be one of the best matches ever played between the two sides. England coming out victors by only one point fifteen points to sixteen .

After leaving university he was working as a chartered accountant for the A & J Robertson Accountancy firm in Edinburgh. At the outbreak of the First World War he responded to the call by first joining the Watsonian Training Corps and then, in September 1914, enlisting in the 9th Royal Scots (The Dandy Ninth, so called because they were the only battalion in the regiment to wear a kilt). He was later commissioned in the 11th Battalion Black Watch. After training at Nigg, Ross-shire, he sailed for France on 1 October 1915. He was transferred once again, this time within the regiment, joining 8th Black Watch as a Lewis-gun officer and in June 1916 was promoted lieutenant. A friend said of him:

> Off the football field he was the most modest and generous of souls, and if one wanted a speedy road to his disfavour, a quotation from the plentiful 'journalese' spent on his achievements on the field made the genial 'Puss' depart from his geniality. That boyish smile, with which he would emerge from the feet of opposing forwards, was an open sesame to a wide circle of friendships, and never could it be said of him that success had in the least turned his head. He was ever sunny, modest and gentle.

Puss Milroy was killed in action at Delville Wood on 18 July 1916. His body was never discovered and he is commemorated on the Thiepval Memorial in France.

## International Caps

5 February 1910. Wales (8) 14 vs Scotland (0) 0. National Stadium, Cardiff.

18 March 1911. England (8) 13 vs Scotland (3) 8. Twickenham.

3 February 1912. Wales (7) 21 vs Scotland (3) 6. St Helen's, Swansea. (1 try)

24 February 1912. Ireland (7) 10 vs Scotland (3) 8. Lansdowne Road, Dublin.

16 March 1912. Scotland (0) 8 vs England (0) 3. Inverleith.

23 November 1912. Scotland (0) 0 vs South Africa (3) 16. Inverleith.

1 January 1913. France (3) 3 vs Scotland (8) 21. Parc des Princes.

1 February 1913. Scotland (0) 0 vs Wales (3) 8. Inverleith.

22 February 1913. Scotland (18) 29 vs Ireland (5) 14. Inverleith.

15 March 1913. England (3) 3 vs Scotland (0) 0. Twickenham.

28 February 1914. Ireland (0) 6 vs Scotland (0) 0. Lansdowne Road, Dublin.

21 March 1914. Scotland (3) 15 vs England (3) 16. Inverleith.

**Captain Thomas Arthur Nelson**
**1st Lothians and Border Horse**
**Died 9 April 1917**
**Aged 40**
**Centre**
**One Cap**

*'Ungrudgingly spontaneously, in the cause of Right, of King, and of Empire'*

Thomas Arthur Nelson was born in 1876, the first son of Thomas Nelson, Publisher, and Jessie Kemp Nelson, of St Leonards, Dalkeith Road, Edinburgh. He was educated at the Edinburgh Academy (1887-95) and at University College, Oxford (1895-99). Nelson was the full back of the Academy XX during the season 1893/94, and a centre three-quarter in the seasons 1894 and 1895. While at Oxford he got his blue in 1897; he played for Oxford as a centre three-quarter against Cambridge on two occasions and was on the winning side both times.

In 1898 he was selected to play in the Calcutta Cup match for Scotland. The match, played at Powderhall, Edinburgh in front of a crowd of eighteen thousand, was drawn three-three. After finishing his studies he became a partner in his father's firm of publishers, Thomas Nelson and Sons. He became a JP for Argyllshire, a lieutenant in the Lothians and Borders Horse Yeomanry, and a member of the King's Body Guard for Scotland (Royal Company of Archers). During this time he even found time to marry Margaret, the third daughter of Alex Balfour of Mount Alyn, Denbighshire.

He travelled with his regiment to France in September 1915. Promoted captain in 1916 he became an intelligence officer and, in 1917, was transferred to the Tank Corps. Off the field or on it, he was a most popular man, and, to judge him only by his many patriotic actions since war had broken out, a most public-spirited one as well. How magnificently he fought, the military records clearly prove as, between 3 April 1916 and 9 April 1917, he was Mentioned in Despatches on no fewer than three occasions, namely 30 April 1916, 13 November 1916 and 9 April 1917, the last occasion being for his brave work on the day of his death. It was while attached to the Tank Corps as an observation officer that he was killed by a shell on 9 April 1917. A friend wrote of him:

He left Oxford to take his part in the great publishing house which bears his name. He worked hard at the business, and under his hands and those of his colleagues it grew to be perhaps the largest organization of its kind in the world. But his life could not be narrowed to one interest. No employer ever gave more thought to the well-being of his employees, and no master ever enjoyed a more whole-hearted popularity. He had a deep interest in all schemes of social betterment, and, being too modest to preach, he was content to practise. He was a keen Yeomanry officer, a pioneer of afforestation, an ideal West Highland laird. He was the best of sportsmen, not merely because he did everything well and with immense gusto, but because he had in his bones the love of wild life and adventure and contest. But his great endowment was his genius for friendship with all human classes and conditions. His kind, serious eyes looked out on the world with infinite friendliness and understanding. His death makes a bigger hole in the life of Scotland than that of any man of his years.

His great friend from his Oxford days Colonel John Buchan dedicated his famous book *The Thirty-Nine Steps* to Nelson.

## International Caps
12 March 1898. Scotland (0) 3 vs England (0) 3. Powderhall, Edinburgh.

**Private James (Peary) Pearson**
**9th Bn Royal Scots**
**22 May 1915**
**Aged 26**
**Centre**
**Twelve Caps**

*'Peerless three-quarter, private soldier and gentleman'*

James Pearson was born on 24 February 1889, the second son of William Pearson, a stonemason, and Isabella Pearson, of Scotts Close, Dalkeith (his brothers and sister were William, Robert and Mary). He went to George Watson's College in 1896 and while there began to play cricket for the school, turning out for the first XI between 1904 and 1907 and making his first century (102 not out) in 1907 for a former pupils' XI against Leith Caledonian. During the 1905/06 season he was persuaded by friends to take up rugby and, in his first season, an accident to Eric Milroy (Scottish International, captain of Scotland, twelve caps, killed in action 18 July 1916) saw him get a place in the first XV as a half. The following year he was in the side as a three-quarter, which proved to be his real position. Pearson scored an extraordinary 103 tries for Watsonians during a period when they won the championship four times between 1909 and 1914. In the summer of 1907 he also carried off the school championship at the athletic sports, being placed in the 100 yards, 440, the hurdles, throwing the cricket ball, and the long jump.

After leaving school he played regularly for Watsonians at both cricket and football; he missed only two cricket matches for them, and that was when playing for Edinburgh vs Glasgow, and only missed one rugby match owing to an attack of water on the knee. In seven seasons of Watsonian cricket he won the batting average on either three or four occasions. In 1914 he topped the Watsonians' averages with the highest that had been recorded for fifty-two years. He was very light for an international three-quarter, weighing a little over nine stone which, undoubtedly, held back his international career despite his tenacious play. It was said of him that 'He was nearly a wonderful player'. As a rugby player he went on to represent Scotland on twelve occasions, being on the winning side six times and on the losing side six times. Against France in 1911 he dropped a goal, and again against France in 1912 he dropped a goal from a penalty and scored a try. He also played seven-a-side football, was a keen golfer and an exceptional athlete who won numerous races, and played tennis, badminton, fives, and curling.

At the outbreak of the war he enlisted into the ranks of the 9th Battalion, Royal Scots (in 81 Brigade of 27th Division) becoming Private 2061 Pearson. He left for the front with B Company on his twenty-sixth birthday, 24 February 1915. James Pearson was killed by a sniper while going along the back of his trench for water during fighting in Sanctuary Wood, in Ypres, on 22 May 1915. A comrade remembered hearing of his death:

> Late in the afternoon word came down from the trenches and passed like wildfire that Pearson, the Rugby International and the most notable of men still remaining in the ranks of the Ninth, had been killed.

In 1930, a comrade wrote:

> Sanctuary Wood has many memories, but there is one which transcends all others – the sight of the wee white face with the little smile as we filed past the little athlete lying in his last long sleep, clad not in the panoply of greatness which he deserved, but in the common tunic and kilt of a private lying like a warrior taking his rest. ... His name was known and loved by thousands. Countless times he had thrilled them with his genius, and now, in the sacred cause, he had laid down his life as a humble soldier. Never again will the little round-shouldered figure, with its long arms and gloved hands, gather a ball unerringly as of yore; but there must always be one spot in Sanctuary Wood that is for ever hallowed in Scottish rugger hearts – the resting place of Jimmy P, peerless three-quarter, private soldier and gentleman.

He is buried in Sanctuary Wood Cemetery, Ieper, West-Vlaanderen, Belgium (Grave VE. 27).

## International Caps

27 February 1909. Scotland (3) 9 vs Ireland (0) 3. Inverleith.

20 March 1909. England (8) 8 vs Scotland (3) 18. Athletic Ground, Richmond.

22 January 1910. Scotland (11) 27 vs France (0) 0. Inverleith.

5 February 1910. Wales (8) 14 vs Scotland (0) 0. National Stadium, Cardiff.

26 February 1910. Ireland (0) 0 vs Scotland (3) 14. Balmoral Showgrounds, Belfast.

19 March 1910. Scotland (5) 5 vs England (5) 14. Inverleith.

2 January 1911. France (11) 16 vs Scotland (8) 15. Stade Olympique, Paris.

20 January 1912. Scotland (13) 31 vs France (3) 3. Inverleith.

3 February 1912. Wales (7) 21 vs Scotland (3) 6. St Helen's, Swansea.

23 November 1912. Scotland (0) 0 vs South Africa (3) 16. Inverleith.

22 February 1913. Scotland (18) 29 vs Ireland (5) 14. Inverleith.

15 March 1913. England (3) 3 vs Scotland (0) 0. Twickenham.

**Captain Lewis Robertson**
**Cameron Highlanders**
**Died 3 November 1914**
**Aged 31**
**Nine Caps**
**Forward**

*'Chevalier sans peur et sans reproch'*
*(The knight without fear and beyond reproach)*

Robertson was born on 4 August 1883, at Hawthornden, the youngest son of James Robertson, wine merchant of 7 Eglinton Crescent, Edinburgh. He was educated at Cargilfield Preparatory School, Edinburgh, before moving up to Fettes College in the same city. While at Fettes he played for the first XV but there seems to be some doubt as to whether he got his colours. In December 1901 he moved onto the Royal Military College, Sandhurst, passing out with Honours in 1902 and was commissioned in the 1st Battalion Queen's Own Cameron Highlanders in May 1903 then at Fort George. Robertson moved to Dublin with his battalion in 1905 where he began to play for Monkstown. In 1911 he was appointed Assistant Inspector of Gymnasia to Eastern Command, stationed at Shorncliffe. During this time, however, he never missed an opportunity to play rugby. His friend Major H. C. Harrison RMA (Old Edwardians, United Services, Navy, Army and England) said of him:

> He was quite the hardest man to come up against I ever met on the football field. He used to go through every game with teeth clenched, often muttering to himself to spur him on. He was a terror to run up against, as hard as a nail and a fighter through and through, until he was absolutely stopped.

Robertson was a man who just loved the game. Not only did he play for Monkstown, but also for United Services, Edinburgh Wanderers, London Scottish (ten Seasons), Fettesian, Lorettonians and six successive years for the Army and Navy at Queen's Club. He was also captain of the Army XV side that beat the Navy in March 1914. His great friend and player Major Rainsford-Hannay DSO wrote about Robertson:

> Lewis Robertson was one of my great friends. My youngest boy, who was born on August 23rd 1914, is called after him, and he was to have been his godfather. As

regards any details of his soldiering life I can tell you very little. I do know that he was shot through the shoulder, and insisted on going back to his company after the wound had been dressed. He was then wounded again, this time mortally. He could not be taken away, and had to be left where he was till night. He talked and spoke quite cheerfully after being hit the second time. He died at, I think, the Convent of the Blessed Virgin, Ypres and is buried in the garden ... If I had to write his epitaph, I think I could do it in four words: 'a very perfect gentleman.'

Robertson played twice at Bordeaux with the Army XV. During the years 1908 to 1913 he played nine times for Scotland, playing his first international in March 1908 and his next in February 1911. In February 1912 (in Edinburgh) he played in the most disastrous defeat Scotland ever sustained against Wales, that of three goals (one dropped) and six tries to one dropped goal and two tries. He continued to play in every match of 1912, including that against the South Africans on 23 November and all three of the Home Unions in 1913, his last international being the 'close call' at Twickenham which England won by a try to nil.

He was promoted to lieutenant in 1909 and at the outbreak of war was sent to France arriving, on 26 September 1914. He took part in the battle of the Aisne, was gazetted captain on 16 January 1915 (to date from 30 September 1914) and died of wounds on 3 November 1914.

Captain Lewis Robertson was initially buried in the gardens of the Blessed Virgin in Wennick Street, Ypres. Later, however, his body was removed and is now buried in Ypres Reservoir Cemetery (Grave II.A.4).

It was said that to all that knew him he was 'Chevalier sans peur et sans reproch' (the knight without fear and beyond reproach).

No man who knew him on or off the field will dare question his right to that.

## International Caps

21 March 1908. Scotland (7) 16 vs England (10) 10. Inverleith.

4 February 1911. Scotland (4) 10 vs Wales (7) 32. Inverleith.

3 February 1912. Wales (7) 21 vs Scotland (3) 6. St Helen's, Swansea.

24 February 1912. Ireland (7) 10 vs Scotland (3) 8. Lansdowne Road. Dublin.

16 March 1912. Scotland (0) 8 vs England (0) 3. Inverleith.

23 November 1912. Scotland (0) 0 vs South Africa (3) 16. Inverleith.

1 February 1913. Scotland (0) vs Wales (3) 8. Inverleith.

22 February 1913. Scotland (18) 29 vs Ireland (5) 14. Inverleith.

15 March 1913. England (3) 3 vs Scotland (0) 0. Twickenham.

**75027 Sergeant Andrew Ross**
**29th (British Columbia Regiment) Bn Canadian**
**Expeditionary Force**
**Died 6 April 1916**
**Aged 37**
**Five Caps**
**Forward**

*'A man feels it's worth his while giving up his life to save millions'*

Andrew Ross was born on 15 May 1879 in Edinburgh, the eldest surviving son of Andrew Ross and was educated at Mr Henderson's private school in Edinburgh before attending the Royal High School. He excelled at games and was noted as a good all-round athlete and swimmer. At sixteen he left school and was apprenticed on the *Glenfyne,* sailing from Dundee. After rounding the Horn his wanderlust seemed to leave him for a while and he returned to school to complete a further year. After this he became apprenticed to a firm of engineers and while with them played for the former pupils' team of his old school. A courageous and fast forward, he quickly came to note and in 1899 played in the Inter-City game for Edinburgh against Glasgow. Glasgow was expected to win as they had during the previous ten seasons. However, on 2 December 1899, all that changed and the Edinburgh pack, including Andrew Ross, defeated Glasgow.

After completing his apprenticeship, Ross once again returned to sea. He became a marine engineer and travelled the world, becoming involved in numerous adventures, nearly dying of yellow fever in Rio and narrowly escaping a 'diabolical' plot when a trap door failed to work. In Cuba he played the bagpipes to an astonished audience. He finally arrived home in 1904 and played again in the Inter-City at Hamilton Crescent, Glasgow, Edinburgh winning six-three. On the same day he was chosen to play for the Cities vs Rest, and his abilities in that game, played on 14 January 1905, led to him being chosen to play for Scotland against Wales at Inverleith on 4 February 1905. Unfortunately, Wales won by two tries to one. Ross remained with the side for the meeting against Ireland which took place on 25 February 1905, once again at Inverleith. Ireland won by one goal and two tries to one goal, the Irish backs proving too strong for the Scottish backs. However, Scotland went on to win the next match against England eight points to nil at Richmond. Ross had one rib broken and two cracked early in the match, but despite this he stuck it out until the end before catching the night mail home. Once at home, and clearly in pain, his family called the doctor. After giving Ross a stern lecture, the doctor forced him to remain in bed for several weeks.

Four years later on 6 February 1909 he was in the Scottish team once again, this time against Wales at Inverleith. Scotland lost by a goal to a penalty goal. On 27 February 1909 he represented Scotland again, this time against Ireland, losing by a penalty goal to nil. It was Ross's last international match. After working as an assistant engineer for the Edinburgh Municipal Electric Station, he moved to Canada, settling in Vancouver. Ross was within the Arctic Circle when war was declared but made his way south quickly to join up. From his own correspondence dated 29 November 1914: 'We arrived in Vancouver from Albert Bay on the 14th of this month, and have started training ... In this Second Canadian Contingent most of the men are splendid shots ...'

There was never a dull moment on Ross's section of the line. On 23 November 1915 he wrote again:

We got a prisoner the other day who told us that London was in ruins, and that Great Britain was starving for want of food. We couldn't get grain into the country, as the Kaiser's submarines had command of the sea, and there were going to be big riots all over England and Scotland ...

Ross met his death on 6 April 1916. A corporal in his company wrote this letter:

On the morning of the 6th April we were serving together in the trenches. While attending devotedly and most courageously, under heavy artillery fire, to our wounded men he himself was hit, and falling over a man he was dressing, died instantly.

It was discovered later that Ross had already been wounded but continued to dress his wounded friend until killed himself.

Sergeant Andrew Ross is buried in Ridge Wood Military Cemetery, Belgium (Grave I.R.9).

## International Caps

4 February 1905. Scotland (3) 3 vs Wales (3) 6. Inverleith.

25 February 1905. Scotland (0) 5 vs Ireland (5) 11. Inverleith.

18 March 1905. England (0) 0 vs Scotland (0) 8. Athletic Ground, Richmond.

6 February 1909. Scotland (0) 3 vs Wales (0) 5. Inverleith.

27 February 1909. Scotland (3) 9 vs Ireland (0) 3. Inverleith.

**2565 Private James (Jimmy) Ross**
**14th Bn The London Regiment (London Scottish)**
**Died 31 October 1914**
**Aged 34**
**Forward**
**Five Caps**

*'Grief was indeed great and hearts heavy'*

James Ross was born on 15 February 1880 at Rutherford, Roxburgh, the son of Richard Ross and was educated at Cargilfield Trinity, Edinburgh (1888-1894), and Fettes College Edinburgh (1894-1899), where he carried off several prizes, and was in the rugby XV (captain 1897, 1898 and 1899).

In 1899, when he left school, he joined the firm of Renton Brothers and Company, becoming a member of the Stock Exchange in 1905. He played numerous games for the London Scottish Rugby Club, which he captained in 1901/02 and 1904/05. In 1901 to 1903 he had won his Scottish international caps as a forward, playing against England, Ireland and Wales. Ross was described as being sturdily built, very hard working and of the 'short heavy type.'

At the outbreak of the war 'Jimmy,' despite his background, enlisted into the ranks of the 14th Battalion The London Regiment (The London Scottish) and went with them to France during the first few months of the war. The London Scottish became the first Territorial Force unit to see action in First World War, when they filled a breach in the line close to Messines at the end of October 1914. Packed into thirty-four London buses, the 1st Battalion London Scottish arrived at Ypres at 3 am on 29 October 1914. After being moved about a little the battalion set off for Messines Ridge where an opening had been forced in the Allied front line. Their task was to reinforce the Allied line and close the opening near what were known as Hun's Farm and Middle Farm. At the time Messines Ridge was occupied by the British infantry and was under heavy artillery fire.

Twice the London Scottish not only halted German attacks but also forced the Germans back from the ridge, despite the fact that they were in an open position, faced overwhelming odds, and were forced to make do with malfunctioning weapons and ammunition. A third attack saw the German troops break through the London Scottish defences, leaving the battalion with heavy casualties and cut off from headquarters. To avoid total destruction of the battalion, orders were given for a retreat towards Wulvergem. German forces had also suffered severe losses, however, and were therefore unable to hinder the London Scots' retreat. Later in the day the battalion regrouped at Kemmel and moved on to the Clytte.

Although the ridge was captured by the Germans, the efforts of the London Scottish had gained time and ultimately prevented the German army breaking through to Ypres. Their bravery and determination had cost the Scots 394 of the 700 officers and men who went into action. Unfortunately, the gallant Ross was among the missing presumed killed during that very gallant action.

He is commemorated on the Ypres (Menin Gate) Memorial, Ieper, West-Vlaanderen, Belgium (Panel 54).

Remarks: His brother Edward Ross (Indian Army) was capped for Scotland in 1904.

## International Caps

9 February 1901. Scotland (10) 18 vs Wales (0) 8. Inverleith.

23 February 1901. Scotland (9) 9 vs Ireland (5) 5. Inverleith.

9 March 1901. England (0) 3 vs Scotland (15) 18. Rectory Field, Blackheath.

1 February 1902. Wales (14) 14 vs Scotland (5) 5. National Stadium, Cardiff.

21 March 1903. England (3) 6 vs Scotland (7) 10. Athletic Ground, Richmond.

**Lieutenant Ronald Francis Simson**
**Royal Field Artillery**
**Died 14 September 1914**
**Aged 24**
**Centre**
**One Cap**

*'A fine character and a wonderful player'*

Ronald Francis Simson was born in Edinburgh on 6 September 1890 and educated at the Edinburgh Academy from 1897 to 1909. Choosing a career in the Army, he entered the Royal Military Academy, Woolwich in 1909. He was in the Academy XV (captain 1909) and the XI. He was a keen athlete, winning the Calcutta Cup for athletics when he came first in the 100 yards, the hurdles, the quarter mile, and the high and long jumps. At Woolwich he was in the XV and won the silver bugle for athletics, taking the hurdles, quarter and the long jump. He played for the Army against the Navy at Queen's Club in 1911 to 1913, his impressive appearance in 1911 securing for him his first international cap for Scotland as a centre three-quarter against England, when Scotland lost by a goal and a try to two goals and a try, Simson scoring one of the Scots' tries.

Why he was overlooked for Scotland in 1912, 1913 and 1914 is a mystery to most. None who took his place were better all-round players than he, if indeed his equal. Despite only being picked once for Scotland, he often played for London Scottish and for the United Services.

It was said of him, by a friend:

'Ronnie' Simson, for so everyone called him at school was a universal favourite. The ordinary Scottish boy is reserved and hates to show his feelings. He seems rather ashamed to smile and only does it under provocation. But 'Ronnie' was quite different; he was bubbling over with mirth … if he was stamped on by the opposing forwards, he came up shaking with laughter.

He left with his battery for France in August 1914 and was quickly involved in some of the heaviest fighting (16 Battery, XLI Brigade, 2nd Division). On 14 September 1914 Simson was riding forward as reconnoitring officer, to select a new position for his battery, when a shell burst right under his horse, killing both. After his death a brother officer wrote:

> It is not by any means because he was the first Rugby International killed in this war that R. F. Simson will be long remembered. It is because he was a fine character and a wonderful player. To watch him play was a sheer delight.

He is buried in Moulins New Communal Cemetery, Aisne, France (Grave 2).

Simson was the first international casualty from the four home teams to be killed. The distinction of being the first international killed during the war has to go to the French player, Alfred Mayssonnie, who was killed on 6 September 1914. Mayssonnie was capped three times for France playing fly or scrum-half.

## International Caps

18 March 1911. England (8) 13 vs Scotland (3) 8. Twickenham.

**Lieutenant Stephen Sebastian Lombard (Beak) Steyn**
**B Battery, 117th Brigade Royal Field Artillery**
**Died 8 December 1917**
**Aged 28**
**Wing**
**Two Caps**

*'He always saw the funny side, and was in consequence a capital man to have in the team'*

Stephen Sebastian Lombard Steyn was born on 10 November 1889, the son of Margret Fraser Steyn, of Cape Province, South Africa and the late Dr Steyn (cousin of President Steyn of the Orange Free State). Steyn was educated first at the Diocesan College, Rondebosch, before going up to University College, Oxford as a Rhodes scholar in 1909. A good all-rounder he played both rugby and cricket for his college.

He was probably a better player as a wing three-quarter during the season 1910/11 than at any other time. In a very odd turn of events, Steyn was chosen to play for Scotland while being overlooked for his university side. However, he always saw the funny side, and was in consequence a capital man to have in the team.

He first played for Scotland against England on 18 March 1911 in the first Calcutta match ever played at Twickenham. Finally, nine months after representing Scotland, he received his blue and played on the winning side against Cambridge. He played on one more occasion for Scotland, this time against Ireland on 24 February 1912, and once more for Oxford against South Africa. Although South Africa was expected to win comfortably, it was in fact a near run thing. They say this was mostly due to the fact that both Steyn and the South African L. R. Broster both understood Dutch and were aware of everything the South Africans were saying and planning. After leaving Oxford Steyn went on to study medicine at Guy's hospital, in 1913, representing their XV on numerous occasions. It is sad to consider that also playing alongside Steyn in the varsity side of December 1912 were W. P. Green, killed in action 1915, E. F. Boyd, killed in action 1914 and W. M. Dickson, killed in action 1915 as well as G. B. Crole, who became a prisoner of war in 1917, and E. G. Loudon-Shand, wounded in both 1915 and 1917.

On 27 October 1910 Steyn joined King Edward's Horse as Private 185 Steyn. In August 1914 he was serving with C Squadron at Watford and was promoted lance corporal before accepting a commission in the Royal Artillery in November 1914.

After training he embarked for France on 20 September 1915. In December of that year, after only a few months in France, he was posted to Salonika. After recovering from a severe bout of typhoid fever he was reunited with his battery. In September 1917 he embarked with the battery for Egypt. He was killed in action in Palestine on 8 December 1917, the day before Jerusalem fell to General Allenby's forces, and was buried in a temporary grave.

In 1920 his body was exhumed and taken to the Jerusalem War Cemetery, Israel, (Grave B. 12) where he now rests.

## International Caps
18 March 1911. England (8) 13 vs Scotland (3) 8. Twickenham.
24 February 1912. Ireland (7) 10 vs Scotland (3) 8. Lansdowne Road, Dublin.

**Second Lieutenant Walter Riddell Sutherland
(Wattie Suddie)
Seaforth Highlanders
Died 4 October 1918
Aged 27
Wing
Thirteen Caps**

*'The barest truth is that he never played a poor game'*

Walter Riddell Sutherland was born on 19 November 1890, the son of Alexander and Isabella Sutherland, of the Imperial Hotel, Hawick, Roxburgh. He was educated at the Teviot Grove Academy before taking up training as a sanitary inspector in the office of the Burgh Engineer, Hawick. He had always shown an aptitude for sports and had done well while at school in a variety of sports, including the school's cricket and football teams. He was also an extremely fast track runner and was the Scottish Border Champion at several distances. He represented Scotland against Ireland in 1911 to 1913 and defeated the Irish champion.

After leaving school he joined the famous Hawick Greens, a team within whose ranks were players such as R. H. Lindsay-Watson, William Burnet and Willie Kyle. He quickly came to notice as a good and reliable three-quarter back. He also became a prolific goal scorer: during the 1909/10 season he scored thirteen tries and kicked twelve goals; in 1910/11 he scored sixteen tries; in 1911/12 he scored twenty-one tries and kicked eight goals; in 1912/13 he scored fourteen goals and in 1913/14 eight tries in eleven games.

With his extraordinary talent and goal-scoring ability he was quickly chosen to represent his country, an honour he achieved on no less than thirteen occasions, including the famous meeting between South Africa and France. It was in the English game at Twickenham in 1913 that Sutherland proved his worth. In direct opposition was the brilliant English centre Ronnie Poulton of Oxford and Harlequins. This powerful Cambridge University wing was considered by many to be the greatest three-quarter back of all time. In 1913 Poulton's rugby prowess was summed up:

R. W. Poulton's brilliant play in the rugby international matches has been a feature of the past football season. We sympathise with the unfortunate man who on being reproved for not stopping him, replied, 'How can anybody stop him when his head goes one way, his arms another, and his legs keep straight on?'

Early in the 1913 match at Twickenham, the Scottish and Oxford University centre Eric Louden-Shand was injured. Reduced to a mere passenger, he moved to Sutherland's position on the wing and Sutherland moved to centre. Of the subsequent contest between Sutherland and Palmer, 'Jock' Wemyss wrote:

What 'Suddie' accomplished in that game was not one miracle but repeated miracles. Time and again when England attacked, he challenged Poulton. He never let him through. He made him pass or be tackled. Then when Poulton passed, and although Louden-Shand was hopelessly crippled and could give no assistance, 'Suddie's' great speed enabled him to get across to tackle Coates and never once did the big winger get clear.

At the outbreak of war Sutherland was one of the first to join up. In September 1914 he joined the Lothians and Border Horse Yeomanry, transferring to the 14th Battalion Argyll and Sutherland Highlanders the following July and proceeding with them to France in May 1916. Sutherland applied for a commission and was gazetted second lieutenant in 8th Seaforth Highlanders. He soon became involved in the fighting, including the affair at Buzancy where 15th (Scottish) Division covered itself with glory. In a letter home to his father he revealed that he was one of only four officers out of eighteen to emerge from the battle.

Sutherland was killed trying to reach his men on 4 October 1918, just over a month before the war ended. He had borrowed a bike during a rest period for his battalion and was making his way back to them when a stray shell exploded next to him in the village of Hulluch, killing him instantly.

Probably the finest tribute paid to Sutherland was by Mr Walter Hume, Headmaster of Trinity School, Hawick:

It is not, however, the enumeration of his brilliant deeds on the football and athletic field that forms the chief claim to the high esteem in which Walter Sutherland was held. He stood for all that was best in whatever he did ... He had no occasion to resort to trick or stratagem; his play was, like his life, clean and wholesome ... By so many lovable ties had he endeared himself to the followers of the Rugby game, and his death was looked upon as a personal loss. For those of us that had followed his career, and had watched his development, it is hard to realize that one who so recently had walked the old Border town, who was held in such affection by its youth, whose bright smile and cheery nature were like rays of sunshine, had gone and would never again adorn its peaceful life ... The memory of such a life, with so many just claims to remembrance, will always stand out as a permanent inspiration and a bright example to all who may follow the Rugby game.

He is buried in Houchin British Cemetery, Pas de Calais, France (III C.22).

## International Caps

5 February 1910. Wales (8) 14 vs Scotland (0) 0. National Stadium.

19 March 1910. Scotland (5) 5 vs England (5) 14. Inverleith.

2 January 1911. France (11) 16 vs Scotland (8) 15. Stade Olympique, Paris.

18 March 1911. England (8) 13 vs Scotland (3) 8. Twickenham.

20 January 1912. Scotland (13) 31 vs France (3) 3. Inverleith. 2 tries.

3 February 1912. Wales (7) 21 vs Scotland (3) 6. St Helen's, Swansea.

16 March 1912. Scotland (0) 8 vs England (0) 3. Inverleith. 1 try

23 November 1912. Scotland (0) 0 vs South Africa (3) 16. Inverleith.

1 January 1913. France (3) 3 vs Scotland (8) 21. Parc des Princes.

1 February 1913. Scotland (0) 0 vs Wales (3) 8. Inverleith.

22 February 1913. Scotland (18) 29 vs Ireland (5) 14. Inverleith.

15 March 1913. England (3) 3 vs Scotland (0) 0. Twickenham.

7 February 1914. Wales (7) 24 vs Scotland (5) 5. National Stadium. Cardiff.

**Lieutenant Frederick Harding (Tanky) Turner**
**10th Bn King's Liverpool Regiment**
**Died 10 January 1915**
**Aged 27**
**Captain/Flanker**
**Fifteen Caps**

*'Never have I met a truer, straighter man than he, or one braver or more modest'*

Frederick Harding Turner was born on 29 May 1888 at Sefton Park, Liverpool. He was educated at Greenbank, at Sedbergh School, Yorkshire between 1902 and 1907, where he was captain of football and cricket. In 1907 he went up to Trinity College, Oxford and remained there until 1910, becoming captain of the first XV. A first class all-round sportsman, he played against Cambridge between 1908 and 1910, having no lesser a man than R. W. Poulton, a future captain of England, in his side. He also picked up the nickname 'Tanky' because of his physical size and robustness.

After leaving University Turner worked for his father's printing firm, Turner & Dunnett. He also went on to represent Scotland fifteen times. He played against England, Ireland, Wales and France in every match of the three seasons 1911 to 1913, against the South Africans in 1912 and again against England and Ireland in 1914, gaining fifteen caps in all and becoming captain of Scotland in 1914.

Turner was in business in Liverpool when war broke out. He was commissioned lieutenant in the 10th Battalion The King's Liverpool Regiment (Liverpool Scottish), and left for the front on 1 November 1914.

He later wrote from the front:

> We are not yet the finest battalion in the British Army, nor have we absolutely annihilated the Prussian Guard; all we have really done is to take our share in the discomforts and in some of the dangers of the campaign without grousing.

Turner was shot and killed by a sniper in the trenches near Kemmel on 10 January 1915. A fellow officer later outlined the circumstances of his death:

> Freddy had been putting some barbed wire out in front of the trench, and after breakfast he went down to have a look at the position. Twice he was shot at when he looked up for a second. He then got to a place where the parapet was rather

low, and was talking to a sergeant when a bullet went between their heads. Freddy said, 'By Jove, that has deafened my right ear,' and the sergeant said, 'and my left one too sir'. He then went a shade lower down and had a look at the wire, and was shot clean through the middle of the forehead, the bullet coming out at the back of his head, killing him instantly. The same man had evidently been following him all the way down the trench, and he ought not to have looked up for a bit, as a man walking along a trench can be seen by the enemy every time he passes a loophole. We got him down to --------- that night with great difficulty and buried him in the local churchyard in the pouring rain. The grave, though baled out in the evening, was 18inches deep in water. However, it is quite the best cared-for grave in the churchyard, and looks very pretty, with a nice cross put up by one of the other regiments in the brigade, and also a nice wreath.

Lieutenant. R. W. Poulton-Palmer on hearing of the death of his club and University captain wrote:

The death of F. H. Turner has been a sad blow to his many friends, and to one unused to writing character sketches it is indeed hard to put down on paper the effect that his cheering presence had upon those with whom he was acquainted. Thousands of those who have watched his play in Varsity, club, and International matches must have realized the strength he was to his side, quite apart from his own individual effects, which were a very high standard. I have played behind many packs of forwards, but never have I been so free from anxiety as when those forwards were led by Fred Turner. Those who saw last year's England v Scotland match could realize what an anxiety to his opponents his peculiarly infectious power of leading was. His play, like his tackle, was hard and straight, and never have I seen him the slightest bit perturbed or excited; and in this fact lay the secret of his great power and control. His kicking ability is well known, and his tenacious determination to stick it was well shown in the Varsity match of 1909, when he returned to help his scrum when in great pain, with one knee useless owing to a displaced cartilage. Off the field he was the same. Whether one saw him at his home, at his old school, at the Varsity, or walking on the hills, his face always showed his cheery satisfaction with the world at large. At any moment he would burst into that cheery and infectious laugh. He was always ready to take part in any harmless practical joking, on tour or elsewhere. His loss is part of the heavy burden of war: and England, in defending her Honour, will have to face the loss of the very best of her sons.

Lieutenant Frederick Harding Turner is buried in Kemmel Churchyard (Special Memorial 13). The church is situated at Heuvelland, West-Vlaanderen, Belgium.

# Scotland

## International Caps

2 January 1911. France (11) 16 vs Scotland (8) 15. Stade Olympique, Paris.

4 February 1911. Scotland (4) 10 vs Wales (7) 32. Inverleith.

25 February 1911. Scotland (3) 10 vs Ireland (8) 16. Inverleith.

18 March 1911. England (8) 13 vs Scotland (3) 8. Twickenham.

20 January 1912. Scotland (13) vs France (3) 3. Inverleith

3 February 1912. Wales (7) 21 vs Scotland (3) 6. St Helen's, Swansea.

24 February 1912. Ireland (7) 10 vs Scotland (3) 8. Lansdowne Road, Dublin. 1 try.

16 March 1912. Scotland (0) 8 vs England (0) 3. Inverleith.

23 November 1912. Scotland (0) 0 vs South Africa (3) 16. Inverleith.

1 January 1913. France (3) 3 vs Scotland (8) 21. Parc des Princes.

1 February 1913. Scotland (0) 0 vs Wales (3) 8. Inverleith.

22 February 1913. Scotland (18) 29 vs Ireland (5) 14. Inverleith.

15 March 1913. England (3) 3 vs Scotland (0) 0. Twickenham.

28 February 1914. Ireland (0) 6 vs Scotland (0) 0. Lansdowne Road, Dublin.

21 March 1914. Scotland (3) 15 vs England (3) 16. Inverleith.

**Lieutenant Albert Luvian Wade**
**Middlesex Regiment**
**KIA 28 April 1917**
**Aged 32**
**Scrum-half**
**One Cap**

*'Surely one of the best that the great game of*
*Rugby Football has given in old England's cause'*

Albert Luvian Wade was born in Glasgow on 20 September 1884, the son of T. Luvian Wade and educated privately before being sent to Dulwich College (1896-1904). He was in the Dulwich XV between 1902 and 1904 as scrum-half-back and captained the side during the seasons 1902 to 1904. Between 1904 and 1908 he played for the London Scottish and between 1908 and 1913 for the Old Alleynians (captain between 1909 and 1913). He won his one and only cap for Scotland against England on 21 March 1908 at Inverleith, Scotland, winning by three goals (two dropped) and one try to two goals.

At the outbreak of war in August 1914, he joined the 13th Kensingtons. However, on 14 November, he was transferred to the Inns of Court OTC, from where on 15 April 1915 he was given a commission in the 17th Battalion Middlesex Regiment. He was sent to France in September 1915. On 28 March 1916 he was promoted to lieutenant. The following December he was attached to 6 Trench Mortar Battery.

Not only was Bertie Wade a first-class sportsman, he was also a talented black-and-white artist and was never happier than when in the company of the artists in the 'Latin' quarter of his favourite city, Paris. Although the normally spruce-looking Albert seemed out of place mixing with the long-haired, scruffy denizens, when they recognized his talent they took him to their hearts. In a letter to a friend, Wade described his last leave in Paris, 'They all remembered me and all seemed so pleased to see me again, that it fairly brought the tears to my eyes, but then I always was a sentimental ass.'

Personal magnetism and charm of manner were perhaps his greatest assets.

Lieutenant Wade was killed in Action at Oppy Wood, Arras on 28 April 1917. His trench mortar battery had gone well beyond its objective and had actually managed to penetrate into the third line of the German defences, a brave and remarkable achievement. However, a strong German counter-attack not only left Wade dead but stopped his colleagues bringing in his body which was lost to sight and history.

All those who knew him felt his loss keenly. An old Alleynian writing to his father said, 'It is something – it is a great thing – to leave a memory like his, and I hope that the thought of it may comfort you in your deep sorrow.'

Also writing to his father, his great friend and Old Alleynian team mate Stanley H. Cross MC paid the following tribute:

> We were sitting outside our dug out, my company commander and I; the mail from home had just come in, and both of us were deep in the contents of letters and newspapers. 'Haven't I often heard you speak of a great pal of yours named Wade, well-known Rugby man, wasn't he?' I looked up at the sound of Captain T......'s voice, and seeing that he was reading *The Times*, an icy fear stole into my heart as I replied, 'Yes, what's up?' 'Sorry old man, he has gone under; here's a notice about him.' The bright spring afternoon seemed to grow darker at his words, and I went to a quiet spot that I know of, just to have a good think about the best pal I ever had ...

## International Caps

21 March 1908. Scotland (7) 16 vs England (10) 10. Inverleith.

**Lieutenant John George Will**
**Prince of Wales's Own Leinster Regiment (Royal Canadians) & No. 29 Squadron Royal Flying Corps**
**Died 25 March 1917**
**Aged 24**
**Seven Caps**
**Wing**

*'One of the outstanding players among wing three-quarters of this century'*

John George Will was born on 2 September 1892 at Merton in Surrey, the son of Doctor and Mrs Will. After being educated at a private preparatory school and then at Merchant Taylors' School from 1906 to 1911 he went up to Downing College, Cambridge where he remained until 1914.

While at school he played for both the XI (First Year) and the XV in his final three, playing as a stand-off half. He also stood out as an all-round athlete, holding the school record for the quarter mile, as well as being a good long jumper and hurdler. In 1911, during the trials at Cambridge, he played at left wing three-quarter but during his first game against Oxford played stand-off half. During the 1912 and 1913 seasons he played at left wing three-quarter in the inter-varsity and it was in this position that he went on to play for Scotland (with the exception of the match against France in 1914). He was captain elect of Cambridge for 1914 and would have led them out against Oxford in the December had war not been declared.

Will joined the Honourable Artillery Company in August 1914 and went to France with them in September 1914. In March 1915 he took a commission in the Worcesters, transferring to the Leinsters the following April. Will was wounded near Hooge in August of 1915 and later in November of the same year joined the Royal Flying Corps (RFC).

He was posted to Egypt as an observer the same month, returning to England in June 1916 to take his pilot's certificate. During the winter of 1916-17 Will remained in England as an instructor in Dover, being promoted to lieutenant in August 1916. Finally, in February 1917, Will was allowed to return to the front as a fighter pilot with No. 29 Squadron.

# Scotland

Mystery has long surrounded the death of John Will. However, during my research for this book, I think I have finally unravelled it. Wills took off from le Hameau aerodrome at 0825 hours on 25 March 1917. The weather was clear with occasional cloud. He was flying a Nieuport 17, A6751, on an escort mission in company with several other 29 Squadron pilots. It appears that of the five Nieuports that were due to fly on escort duty that day, only three returned. Of those three, Lieutenant T. J. Owen in Nieuport A6721 had to turn back with carburettor problems. Will and Lieutenant C. G. Gilbert in Nieuport A6689 flew on. While on this operation they were attacked by aircraft from Jasta 11 Richthofen's flying circus. Gilbert was shot down by the Red Baron himself and taken prisoner. The only other claim for this action came from the Red Baron's brother, Lothar, who claimed a Nieuport 17 shot down in flames. However, because the location of the crash could not be confirmed, the claim was disallowed. Lother's final score was forty, including Captain Albert Ball VC. It now appears to be forty-one, counting poor Will.

In December 1917 John Will's grave lay in front of a newly advanced British artillery battery. Second Lieutenant Huntley Gordon found a cross made from a broken propeller in front of his gun position, and wrote:

Round the propeller-hub is painted '2nd Lt J G Will RFC'. He was the wing-three quarter known before the war as 'the flying Scot' . . . The grave must have been made by Boche airmen – a curiously chivalrous act, for they can hardly have thought it likely that we would advance far enough to see it.

A friend later wrote of him:

Well do I recall a wonderful try he scored against a representative Swansea team at Cambridge somewhere about 1912. Playing on the left wing as usual, he actually scored the try in the right hand corner. A sight not often witnessed in the case of a match against such a highly combined and well organized team as the First XV of one of the leading Welsh clubs. Will's great pace enabled him to run behind the line of advancing three-quarters, and to take Lowe's pass as though Lowe had been right centre and Will right wing. I remember well the surprise of the opposition, who were considered and not without justice, to be past masters in the art of team defence. There was also a memorable match on the St Helen's Ground, Swansea, when Wales won by 4 goals (2 dropped) and 1 try to Scotland's 2 tries both scored by Will. It was as a result of this match that many people connected to the game commented that they considered Will the best wing in the four Home Unions at that time.

Will is commemorated on the Arras Flying Services Memorial, Pas de Calais, France (Addenda Panel).

## International Caps

20 January 1912. Scotland (13) 31 vs France (3) 3. Inverleith.

3 February 1912. Wales (7) 21 vs Scotland (3) 6. St Helen's, Swansea.

24 February 1912. Ireland (7) 10 vs Scotland (3) 8. Lansdowne Road, Dublin.

16 March 1912. Scotland (0) 8 vs England (0) 3. Inverleith.

7 February 1914. Wales (7) 24 vs (5) 5. National Stadium, Cardiff.

28 February 1914, Ireland (0) 6 vs Scotland (0) 0. Lansdowne Road, Dublin.

21 March 1914. Scotland (3) 15 vs England (3) 16. Inverleith.

**Lieutenant William Middleton Wallace**
**5th Bn Rifle Brigade/No. 2 Squadron Royal Flying**
**Corps**
**Died 22 August 1915**
**Full Back**
**Four Caps**

*'Too Cool, Too Daring'*

William Wallace was born in Edinburgh on 23 September 1892 and educated at Edinburgh Academy from 1899 to 1912 before moving on to King's College, Cambridge where he remained until 15 July 1915. While at the Academy he played full back for their XV, becoming vice captain in 1912, and cricket for the Academy XI (wicket-keeper) becoming captain of the XI in 1911. He won the Bradburn Shield for best all-round athlete in 191, the Burma Cup for the highest number of wins in the school sports of 1912, the fives cup in 1910, was in the gymnasium eight in 1911 and created the school high jump record (5 feet 5 inches) in 1911. Not surprisingly, Wallace was considered to be one of the most versatile schoolboy athletes of his generation.

After going up to King's College, Cambridge he played so well in the Freshmen's match that his place as full back on the varsity side against Oxford in 1912 was assured. In 1913, and despite a serious wrist injury picked up while playing at Newport during the Lent term, he was selected again. With the selectors watching on, Wallace's splendid fielding, long kicking (with either foot) and confident style led to his selection for the national XV of Scotland. He went on to play against England in 1913 and 1914 and against Wales and Ireland in 1914. During these years Wallace was considered to be the best full back in the United Kingdom.

It was said of Wallace that he was too cool, too daring, over confident. That was his way. He did everything, from driving a motor to wicket-keeping, as though nothing mattered and as if nobody was quite as good as he. This was not due to conceit, but to sheer self-confidence of the right type.

Wallace left for France on 11 September 1914, having been gazetted in the Rifle Brigade in August of that year. Wallace saw action with the Rifle Brigade at the battles of the Aisne, Frelinghien and Ploegsteert Wood. Leaving the Rifle Brigade, Wallace became an observer with No. 2 Squadron RFC on 14 February 1915 seeing further action at Neuve Chapelle, Aubers and rue d'Ouvery as well as numerous other actions with the Armentières–la Bassée area. While with No. 2 Squadron Wallace served with the famous William Barnard Rhodes-Moorhouse, who on 26 April 1915 at Kortrijk, Belgium, became the RFC's first ever VC winner. Rhodes-Moorhouse died from his wounds the following day.

By July 1915 Wallace had become the senior observer within his squadron and on 21 July 1915 was promoted to lieutenant. Wallace died while he was engaged in photographic reconnaissance. His plane, a BE 2c, number 2034, being flown by his friend Second Lieutenant Charles Gallie, was shot down by anti-aircraft gunfire, and was said by one eye witness to have fallen like a stone at a place called Sainghin in France. Both men were buried close to their fallen plane. It was said of Wallace that he was the first undergraduate to go into action. Although this would be difficult to prove he certainly would have been one of the first.

His obituary in the Academy *Chronicle* of October 1915 said of him:

His success as an athlete was partly due to his natural ability at all games, but more especially to the inherent qualities of his character. First and foremost, I should put it down to his great self-reliance and coolness – qualities which were apparent in him, not only when playing games, but also in the course of his everyday life … None who ever saw him play will easily forget his beautiful touch-kicking or his reliableness under difficulties; but what impressed the spectator most was the fact that he was always cool and collected, that nothing seemed to put him out, and that he never knew when his side was beaten.

All these qualities are essential in a full back and Wallace possessed them to a high degree. No one who ever saw him play could ever deny that.

After the war Wallace's body together with his pilot Charles Gallie and 3,187 other British and Commonwealth dead were re-interred together at the Cabaret-Rouge British Cemetery, Couchez, their grave number being XII, D.11. The German government later returned his dog tags, together with three photographs and his cigarette case to his father, via the American Embassy.

## International Caps
15 March 1913. England (3) 3 vs Scotland (0) 0. Twickenham.
7 February 1914. Wales (7) 24 vs Scotland (5) 5. National Stadium, Cardiff.
28 February 1914. Ireland (0) 6 vs Scotland (0) 0. Lansdowne Road, Dublin.
21 March 1914. Scotland (3) 15 vs England (3) 16. Inverleith.

**Lieutenant Commander John Skinner Wilson**
**Royal Navy**
**HMS *Indefatigable***
**Died 31 May 1916**
**Aged 32**
**Forward**
**Two Caps**

*'He was thoroughly enthusiastic first and last'*

John Skinner Wilson was born in Trinidad on 10 March 1884, the son of Sir David Wilson KCMG. He was appointed cadet at Britannia Royal Naval College on 15 September 1898 and on 14 January 1900 was gazetted midshipman in *Canopus*, in which he served for three years. He was promoted to acting sub-lieutenant before being promoted lieutenant in January 1905 (with seniority from 10 March 1904), his twentieth birthday. He served in submarines for six months before joining *King Edward VII*, the flagship of Sir Arthur May. In 1906 he joined HMS *Vernon* to specialize in torpedo work. Afterwards he served on HM Ships *Talbot, Formidable, Superb, Dreadnought* and, finally, *Indefatigable* in 1913 as a torpedo-lieutenant.

His love of the game had always been with him. While at Naval College he played for their XV in 1903/04 and in 1907/08, becoming captain during his last two years. He played thirty-three times, winning twenty-eight, losing four and drawing one. This XV also won the Kent County Cup in 1908. He was also captain of the United Services XV in both 1908 and 1909. He played for the Navy against the Army at Queen's in 1907/08 and 1913.

Selected for Scotland he played for them against Ireland in 1908 and Wales in 1909. Those who saw him play described him thus:

> He was a grand forward, one of the busy sort, always to be found somewhere near the ball, and never shirking his bit in the tight work for the sake of splashing about in the open and drawing the plaudits of the easily satisfied.

As in so many cases Wilson didn't just excel at rugby but was a good all-round athlete. He was an especially good oarsman and sailor, winning many races, including the Lord Charles Beresford's Cup for Midshipmen's sailing races.

He was killed in action at the Battle of Jutland on 31 May 1916, when the Indefatigable-class battle-cruiser HMS *Indefatigable* was sunk by gunfire from the SMS *von der Tann* off Jutland. HMS *Indefatigable* had been under fire for about fifteen minutes when, at 0503, it disappeared in a tremendous cloud of black smoke twice the height of her masts. Later two more hits were observed from the following ship, HMS *New Zealand*. Shells pierced the ship's armour and caused massive internal explosions. HMS *Indefatigable* sank with fifty-seven officers and 960 men; two survivors were picked up by the German torpedo-boat S.68.

Lieutenant Commander Wilson is commemorated on the Plymouth Naval Memorial, Devon, United Kingdom (Panel 10).

His elder brother, Major S. Wilson, 1st Royal Munster Fusiliers was killed in action in France.

## International Caps
29 February 1908. Ireland (13) 16 vs Scotland (3) 11. Lansdowne Road Dublin.
6 February 1909. Scotland (0) 0 vs Wales (0) 5. Inverleith.

**Captain Eric Templeton Young**
**Cameronians (Scottish Rifles)**
**Died 28 June 1915**
**One Cap**
**Flanker**

*'A Man of most sincere and straightforward character'*

Eric Templeton Young was born on 14 May 1892. Between 1902 and 1906 he was educated at Cargilfield Preparatory School, Edinburgh before moving up to Fettes College where he was a student from 1906 to 1910. From there he went up to Magdalen College, Oxford where he was an undergraduate from 1910 until 1913. While there he played occasionally for Oxford University but never against Cambridge. Young also played for both Glasgow Academy and Glasgow Academicals. He played his one and only game for Scotland against England in March 1914 at Inverleith in the last international match to be played on British soil before the war. Young had joined the Territorial Force in 1911 and was promoted captain in August 1914. After training at Falkirk, he was sent to Gallipoli with the 8th Battalion Cameronians, sailing from Liverpool on the 24 May 1915 and arriving in Gallipoli (via Egypt) as part of 156 Brigade on 14 June 1915. Two weeks later on 28 June 1915 he was involved in the disastrous attack at Gully Ravine where he was reported missing, presumed killed. During this attack the battalion suffered fourteen officers and 334 other men killed, and a further eleven officers and 114 men wounded. At the end of the action only three officers and seventy men of the battalion were left standing. They had been all but wiped out within two weeks of their first action. A brother officer wrote of him after his death, 'He was a man of most sincere and straightforward character, absolutely downright, and one of the most fearless. He took great interest in his men, and was much loved by them.'

Captain Eric Young has no known grave and is commemorated on the Helles Memorial in Gallipoli together with 20,870 other soldiers who lost their lives in Gallipoli and have no known grave. For many years his name appeared on the le Touret memorial in France together with the names of the 6th Battalion who had been killed in France. However, this mistake was pointed out to the CWGC and they are in the process of placing Young's name on the Helles Memorial.

Perhaps it is best if we leave the last word on Eric Young to Mustafa Kemel Ataturk, the first President of modern Turkey. In a remarkable speech he made on ANZAC Day 1934 he said:

> Those heroes that shed their blood and lost their lives. You are now lying in the soil of a friendly country. Therefore rest in peace. There is no difference between the Johnnies and the Mehmets to us where they lie side by side here in this country of ours. You, the mothers who sent their sons from far away countries, wipe away your tears. Your sons are now living in our bosom and are in peace. Having lost their lives on this land they have become our sons as well.

Eric Templeton Young was one of six Scottish internationals who played in the last game against England in March 1914 and were to lose their lives during the war.

## International Caps
21 March 1914. Scotland (3) 15 vs England (3) 16. Inverleith.

### 1914 Scotland v England

| W. M. Wallace*, | E.T. Young*, | I.M. Pender, | A.W. Symington, | R.M. Scobie, | J.L. Huggan*, |
| J. G. Will*, | C.M. Usher*, | F.H. Turner, | E. Milroy*, | A.W. Angus, | A.R. Ross, | G.H.H.P. Maxwell |
| Players marked * died on active service | | A.D. Laing, | | T.C. Bowie, |

Scotland 1914. (Mistake on photograph, Usher survived the war and Turner was killed)

# South Africa

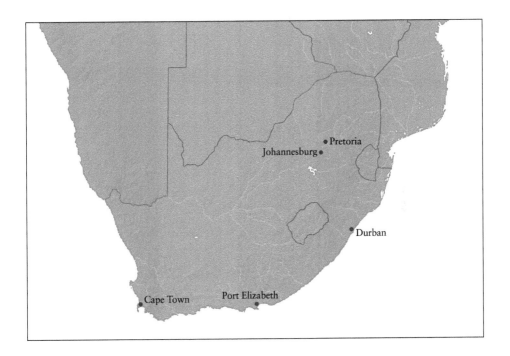

**Captain Adam Francis Burdett**
**South African Service Corps**
**Died 4 November 1918**
**Aged 36**
**South Africa**
**Forward**
**Two Caps**

*Strong, fast and fair, the perfect sportsman*

Adam Francis Burdett was born at Oudtshoorn, South Africa, on 20 August 1882. Educated at the Diocesan College, or Bishops as it is more commonly referred to, in the suburb of Rondebosch, Cape Town, he was described as being five feet ten inches tall, and weighing twelve stone and nine pounds. It was at Bishops that he, like hundreds of other boys, was to learn his rugby. In a school that had turned out more good backs than forwards he was an exception. A good tackler and hard-working forward, he was at his happiest in the open where his clever footwork and pace rendered him both prominent and dangerous.

He went up to Bishop's in 1899 and, starting with the third team, received his senior cap the following year. He played regularly for the school, finally captaining them in 1905. After leaving school in 1906 he was selected to play for the Villagers. However, absence from town kept him out of the team for most of the season. He was also selected to play for Western Province and his form in 1905 was so good that he was picked to play in the tournament at Johannesburg, being really the last man selected for the forward division. He played a good game, but nothing exceptional, and his selection came as somewhat of a surprise. Still, on the tour in England, he had justified his place, playing some really good games, particularly in the Internationals in which he took part.

At the outbreak of the First War he joined up and found himself serving in Tanganyika, German East Africa. While there he contracted malaria from which he never recovered. He was shipped home where he died on 4 November 1918, just seven days before the end of the war. He is buried in Thaba Tshwane (old No.1) Military Cemetery.

**International Matches**
17 November 1906. Scotland (0) 6 vs South Africa (0) Hampden Park, Glasgow.
24 November 1906. Ireland (3) 9 vs South Africa (12) 15. Balmoral Showgrounds, Belfast.

**6004 Sergeant Septimus (Sep) Heyns Ledger**
**2nd Regiment South African Infantry**
**Died 12 April 1917**
**Aged 26**
**Forward**
**Four Caps**

*'He reached all his goals including his final one'*

Septimus Heyns Ledger was born on 29 April 1889, in Kimberley, South Africa, the son of Fred and Elizabeth Ledger (nee Knobel). He attended Kimberley Boys ' High School, Griqualand West, a school that turned out quite a number of excellent rugby players and many internationals and where Ledger quickly developed his talents and played lock.

After leaving school he became a clerk and began to play for Pirates RFC, Griqualand West, at the Hoffe Park Stadium (1912). The rugby team was established in 1886 in the former British colony of Griqualand West. Five years later, during the 1891 British Lions tour to South Africa, Griqualand West played the British in Kimberley, and although they lost three points to nil, the British presented them with the Currie Cup – as they thought that Griqualand West produced the best performance out of the provincial games on their tour. The Currie Cup became South Africa's domestic prize, and Griqualand West first won it in 1899 and subsequently in 1911 (they won it for a third time in 1969).

Sep was chosen to play for South Africa during their 1912/13 tour of the British Isles and France (Springbok number 146). He played fifteen matches in all, four of them internationals, making his test debut against Scotland in Edinburgh on 23 November 1912. His last test appearance was against France on 11 January 1913 in Bordeaux where he scored a try.

At the outbreak of the First World War Sep joined the 2nd Natal Orange Free State Battalion, South African Infantry. This unit was part of the South African Brigade in 9th (Scottish) Division. He landed in France on 25 July 1916, joining his battalion a few days later on the 31st. A natural leader of men and a well-known South African personality he was quickly promoted to sergeant. After seeing some heavy fighting he was killed in action on 12 April 1917. Some records give his date of death as the 13th but I have stuck with the CWGC date of the 12th. An account from the official history of the South Africans in France explains what happened:

> There were two objectives — the first being the road from the inn to the station; and the second, the Chemical Works and buildings south of the railway, the wood called Mount Pleasant, and the village of Roeux. The South African Brigade together with the 27th Brigade were to capture the first objective, after which the 26th Brigade would advance south of the railway.
>
> At 3 p.m. on the 12th the 1st, 2nd, and 4th South African Regiments assembled in Fampoux and were immediately subjected to a heavy and sustained bombardment, which caused many casualties. All three brigades of the 9th Division were very tired, having been hard at work under shell-fire for three days, and having had no sleep for four nights, three of which they had spent lying in the snow without blankets and many without greatcoats. There was no chance of an adequate bombardment, and there was no time to reconnoitre the ground. The country between Fampoux and Roeux station was perfectly open, and was commanded in the south by a high railway embankment and three woods, all of them held by the enemy; while in the north it sloped gradually to the inn around which the Germans had organized strong points. It was impossible, therefore, to prevent the movement of troops being observed by the enemy.
>
> The attack was timed for 5 p.m., when our guns opened fire. Unfortunately our barrage dropped some 500 yards east of the starting-point, and behind the first enemy line of defence, so that the South Africans had a long tract of open ground to cover. Our artillery, too, seemed to miss the enemy machine-gun posts on the railway embankment, which, combined with the flanking fire from the woods and from the direction of the inn, played havoc with both the attacking brigades. The result was a failure. A gallant few of the South Africans succeeded in reaching the station, a point in their objective, where their bodies were recovered a month later when the position was captured. But as a proof of the quality of the troops, it should be recorded that before the attack was brought to a standstill, the casualties of the 2nd Regiment, who went in 400 strong, amounted to 16 officers and 285 men.

Sep Ledger was amongst those dead.

He is commemorated on the Arras Memorial (Bay 10).

## International Caps

23 November 1912. Scotland (0) 0 vs South Africa (3) 16. Inverleith.
30 November 1912. Ireland (0) vs South Africa (12) 38. Lansdowne Road, Dublin.
4 January 1913. England (3) 3 vs South Africa (3) 9. Twickenham.
11 January 1913. France (5) 5 vs South Africa (11) 38. le Bouscat, Bordeaux.

**Captain Tobias (Toby) Mortimer Moll**
**9th Bn Leicestershire Regiment**
**Died 14/15 July 1916**
**Aged 26**
**Forward**
**One Cap**

*'Everything else was impersonal, almost unreal,*
*but with Toby one was up against it'*

Tobias (Toby) Moll was born on 20 July 1890, the son of Tobias and Henrietta Moll of Welbeloond Farm, Potsdam, Cape Province, South Africa. Educated at SACS, where he played prop before going on to play for Hamiltons, he then migrated to the Transvaal where he played for Randfontein as well as for Western Province and Transvaal. Moll was awarded a single cap on 27 August 1910 against the British Isles team during their 1910 tour of South Africa. He was a bank clerk by profession.

At the outbreak of the First World War he joined the 9th Battalion Leicestershire Regiment being commissioned as a second lieutenant; his battalion was in 110 Brigade of 37th Division. Tobias Mortimer Moll died of wounds at the front on 14 or 15 July 1916. An account of his death eventually reached his family in Australia:

> We were now out of that nightmare wood in what was once a village – the village of Bazentin-le-Petit, and the day was 13 July. We had achieved our objective, and fondly believed that the Germans were on their way back to Berlin. We received orders to consolidate. The village was a shambles and nothing remotely resembling a house was to be seen. Here I came across an old friend from Hamilton's, Toby Moll, who told me that Cyril Bam had been killed. No trace of him was to be found. Soon after this, Toby was hit by shrapnel when he was quite near me and I saw at once that there was no hope. It was hard to see Toby go – everything else was impersonal, almost unreal, but with Toby one was up against it.

Tobie Moll is buried in Mericourt-l'Abbe Communal Cemetery Extension, Somme, France (Grave II, D. 5).

## International Caps
27 August 1910. South Africa (3) 3 vs Great Britain (0) 8. Crusaders Ground, Port Elizabeth.

**1455 Private Jan (Jackie) Willem Hurter Morkel**
**1 Mounted Brigade (Van Deventer's Scouts)**
**Mounted Commandos, SA Forces**
**Died 15 May 1916**
**Aged 25**
**Centre**
**Five Caps**

*'He upheld in the worthiest possible manner the teachings of the rugby game …*
*and his case will stand for all time as a shining example to his countrymen'*

Jan (Jackie) Willem Hurter Morkel was born on 13 November 1890 in Somerset West, Cape Province, South Africa, the son of J. and H. Morkel. Jackie Morkel came from one of the most famous rugby-playing families in South Africa. Twenty-one brothers and cousins played first-class rugby in South Africa before the First World War including eight who were, or subsequently became, Springboks. A great all-round sportsman, Morkel not only played rugby union for Western Province but, as a first class, all round sportsman, also represented the Transvaal at cricket.

Jacky Morkel made his debut for the Springboks as an outside centre on the 1912/13 tour of the British Isles and France when he played in all five tests, scoring four tries, including two against Ireland. It was down to his individual brilliance that South Africa narrowly beat the Welsh club side Llanelli. His brother Gerhard Morkel was also on the 1912/13 tour.

When war broke out Jacky enlisted as a trooper in 1 Mounted Brigade, (Van Deventer's Scouts); he was part of the second reinforcements to van Deventer's Scouts. Conditions for troops were not good and medicines were primitive by today's standards and he died on 15 May 1916 of dysentery while serving in East Africa.

He is buried in Dar es Salaam War Cemetery, Tanzania (Grave 5, K. 6), close to his friend and fellow international Tommy Thomson.

## International Caps

23 November 1912. Scotland (0) ) vs South Africa (3) 16. Inverleith.
30 November 1912. Ireland (0) vs South Africa (12) 38. Lansdowne Road, Dublin.
14 December 1912. Wales (0) 0 vs South Africa (3) 3. National Stadium. Cardiff.
4 January 1913. England (3) 3 vs South Africa (3) 9. Twickenham.
11 January 1913. France (5) 5 vs South Africa (11) 38. le Bouscat, Bordeaux.

**3744 Private Gerald W. (Tommy) Thompson**
**5th Regiment South African Infantry**
**Died 20 June 1916**
**Forward**
**Three Caps**

*'Never on a losing side'*

Gerald 'Tommy' W. Thompson was born on 4 October 1886 in Carnarvon, Cape Province, South Africa, the son of Gerald P. T. Thompson. He played hooker/prop Rondebosch Boys' High School in the Western Province. On leaving school he played for the Western Province and was later selected to play for South Africa taking part in the 1912/13 rugby union tour and turning out against Scotland, Ireland, and Wales, being part of the winning side on all three occasions.

On 16 October 1914, shortly after the outbreak of war, he enlisted as a private in the 5th South African Infantry, East Africa Expeditionary Force. In April 1916 he was hospitalized with malaria. On recovering he returned to his regiment and was killed in action at Katanga, East Africa.

He is buried in Dar es Salaam war cemetery in modern Tanzania (8.A.3.), not far from another great South African international, Jacky Morkel.

## International Caps

23 November 1912. Scotland (0) 0 vs South Africa (3) 16. Inverleith.

30 November 1912. Ireland (0) 0 vs South Africa (12) 38. Landsdowne Road, Dublin.

14 December 1912. Wales (0) 0 vs South Africa (3) 3. National Stadium, Cardiff.

# United States of America

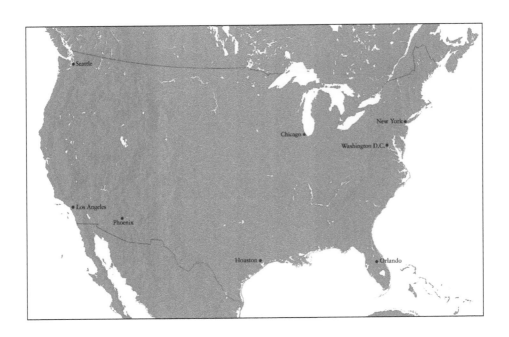

**Lieutenant Frank Jacob (Deke) Gard**
**362nd Infantry Regiment**
**Died 27 September 1918**
**Aged 26**
**Captain/Flanker**
**Two Caps**

Frank Jacob Gard (or Deke as he was affectionately called) was born on 27 March 1892 in Tremont City, Ohio, the eldest son of Emerson Earl Gard and Laura E. (nee Shanley). The family had moved to California in 1905 to become orange growers. Frank was educated at Citrus Union High School, Glendora, and went up to Stanford University in 1910 to read chemistry; while there he was captain of the 1914 American football and rugby sides. His first international was against the Australian touring side, played on 16 November 1912 at California Field, Berkeley in which Deke was a flanker. The USA were winning eight points to six with only minutes to go when the Australians managed to turn the game, coming out winners by twelve points to eight. He represented the USA again, this time against the visiting New Zealanders on 15 November 1913, once more playing flanker. This time the outcome was more decisive, New Zealand coming out ahead by three points to fifty-one. He was also captain of the team on both occasions. Gard graduated in 1914 with a degree in chemistry.

With the 'Old Country' in trouble – the Gard family could trace their roots back to Bideford, Devon, from where they emigrated during the seventeenth century – Frank joined up in June 1917 and became a first lieutenant in the 362nd Infantry Regiment, known as 'The Wild West Division'. He then travelled by ship with his regiment, first to Liverpool and then via Southampton to le Havre, France. He took part in the Meuse-Argonne offensive (the battle of the Argonne Forest) which, up to that time, was the biggest battle ever fought by US troops.

On 26 September 1918 the American First Army attacked the Germans in the broad valley of the River Meuse. Their objective was to capture the Sedan-Mézières railway, an important German transport centre. They took Cheppy Woods, entered Bois de Cheppy before reaching the German positions at la Neuve Grange Farm. After destroying the German machine-gun positions that were causing a high number of casualties they captured the village of Very.

Frank Jacob Gard was killed in action on 27 September 1918 while observing enemy positions. He is buried in Plot B, Row 33, Grave 24, Meuse-Argonne American Cemetery, Romagne, France.

## International Caps
16 November 1912. USA (0) 8 vs Australia (5) 12, California Field, Berkeley.
15 November 1913. USA (3) 3 vs New Zealand (27) 51, California Field, Berkeley.

# Wales

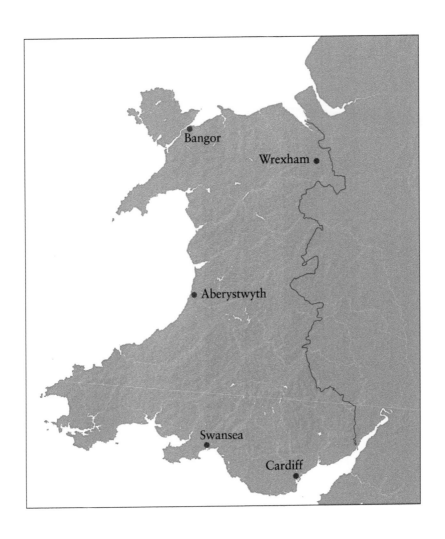

**Lieutenant Colonel Richard Davies Garnons-Williams**
**12th Bn Royal Fusiliers**
**Died 27 September 1915**
**Aged 59**
**Forward**
**One Cap**

*'He would have chosen no other end'*

Richard Davies Garnons-Williams was born on 15 June 1856 at Llowes, Radnorshire, Wales, the second child of the Reverend Garnons-Williams of Abercamlais and Catherine Francis. He was educated at Wimbledon School, Surrey, and Magdalen College, Oxford before moving onto Trinity College, Cambridge in 1874 and the Royal Military College, Sandhurst. He played rugby for both Magdalen College, Oxford and Trinity College, Cambridge yet unusually was never awarded his blue. He also turned out for Sandhurst and played his club football at Newport. In 1881 he was selected by Richard Mullock to play in the first Welsh team in their inaugural match. The team itself was made up from players based more on the geographic spread of clubs they represented and university pedigree than rugby ability. Despite the poor selection process, few were expecting such a disparity in the score line as England humiliated Wales in a one-sided game with England running in thirteen tries. This was Williams's only appearance for Wales. As well as being a first rate rugby player he also excelled at athletics, winning numerous prizes.

On leaving Sandhurst he received his commission in the 1st Battalion Royal Fusiliers on 25 February 1876. He was first posted to the 38th Regiment of Foot (1st Staffordshire Regiment) before being transferred to the 7th Foot (Royal Fusiliers) on 17 February 1877. He served in Gibraltar and Egypt before retiring as a major in 1890. From 1886 to 1892 he was adjutant of the 4th Militia Battalion; during that period he read for and was called to the Bar and also became an active member of the Charity Organization Society. He retired again in 1892, and joined the volunteer battalion of the South Wales Borderers in Brecon, finally becoming a brigade major. In 1909 he became secretary of the National Service League for Brecon, Radnor and Montgomery. In September 1914 he rejoined his old regiment at the age of fifty-eight. After training for a year he

232

was sent out to France in September 1915, second in command of his battalion. He was killed in action on the 27th of that month, the second day of the battle of Loos. A soldier of his battalion later wrote of the action and Williams's death:

> He led his men on September 25th into trenches lately occupied by the Germans and on the 27th the battalion were in a support trench and the furthest they had captured. This trench became untenable and retirement had to be effected to straighten the line, the supports, both right and left having retired, so that their flanks were 'in the air'. As the colonel gave the necessary order to retire and instructions to the machine-gun section to fire over the trench to keep back the Germans, he was shot in the head from an adjoining house and did not move again. I was very sorry for him, as we could not have had a better, braver officer. He was with us all the time in the front trench and looked after us as well as he could; no man could have done better. Nobody could get back to him.

A fellow officer wrote of him, 'He would have chosen no other way.'

He is commemorated on the Loos Memorial to the Missing (Panels 25-27). Colonel Williams was fifty-nine when he was killed, making him the oldest Welsh international to be killed in the Great War.

## International Caps

19 February 1881. England 8G vs Wales 0G. Richardson's Field, Blackheath.

**Second Lieutenant William (Billy) Purdon Geen**
**9th Bn King's Royal Rifle Corps**
**Died 31 July 1915**
**Aged 25**
**Wing**
**Three Caps**

*'He's a heavy loss to Rugger'*

William Purdon Geen, was born at 'Claremont', Gold Tops, Newport, Monmouthshire, Wales, on 14 March 1891, the son of William Rowe (d.1893) Geen and Alicia Geen. He had one older sister, Nora, and was educated at Northam Place, Potter's Bar, Haileybury College, and Oxford. At Haileybury he kept wicket for the XI, and was a first-class centre three-quarter in their XV, becoming their captain in 1910. Geen was also a respectable wicket keeper, playing for Oxford University Authentics and Monmouthshire in the Minor Counties Championship. However it was at rugby that he excelled. He turned out for both Blackheath and the Barbarians and played against the Queen's Club in 1910, 1911, 1912 and 1913 when Oxford won the first two and lost the final two. Although Newport played him as a centre, when he was selected for Wales he played as a wing.

He accepted a commission in the King's Royal Rifle Corps on 21 August 1914 and was sent to Petworth in Sussex for training before embarking for the front in May 1915. The 9th King's Royal Rifles formed part of the 14th Light Division during the Second Battle of Ypres. After over six weeks' hard fighting the battalion was withdrawn for a short period of rest. However, two days later it was ordered back to the front to reinforce 41 Brigade. It was during this fighting that Geen was killed.

Major John Hope wrote of his death:

Geen fought gloriously, and was last seen alive leading his platoon in a charge after being for hours subjected to liquid fire and every device the Germans could bring to bear to break through. Seventeen officers and 333 other ranks of this battalion were killed in this engagement, in which officers and men showed themselves worthy of the best traditions of their Regiment.

On learning of his death an old Haileyburian wrote the following tribute:

234

being dropped from the Welsh squad to face the same South African touring side he had just played against he was recalled for the 1907 Home Nations' Championship. Once again his first match was against England, this time at the St Helen's ground in Swansea. Wales beat England by the impressive margin of twenty-two-nil, Maddock scoring two tries. In their second game, however, they lost to Scotland and Maddock was dropped from the squad, being replaced by Jones in the final game of the campaign, a win at home over Ireland.

Although this seemed to mark the end of Maddock's international career he continued to play for London Welsh, becoming club captain of the senior London Welsh XV. In 1910, three years after being dropped by Wales, he was recalled to the Welsh international team to play in the Five Nations' match against France. Wales beat the French by the remarkable score of forty-nine-fourteen, Wales scoring no less than ten tries with Maddock scoring two of them. Despite the extraordinary victory, and the tries, Maddock was for some reason dropped for the very next game, such are the strange vagaries of selectors. Maddock never represented Wales again but continued playing for London Welsh until 1913.

At the outbreak of the First World War in August 1914 Maddock, along with hundreds of rugby footballers, joined the colours, enlisting on 15 September 1914. He was first posted to the Royal Fusiliers (Public Schools Battalion) before being commissioned into the Machine Gun Corps on 25 September 1916. His natural dash and daring was to earn him a Military Cross on 26 April 1918 for his gallantry in covering the retreat of his unit from les Mesnil. Although practically surrounded, Maddock continued firing until all the men had crossed a bridge and was the last man to retire to safety. He survived the war but, like thousands of other severely wounded men, never recovered fully from injuries sustained on the Somme in 1916 and finally succumbed to those injuries on 21 December 1921 in Cardiff at the young age of forty. The last game of 1921 saw the London Welsh players wearing black armbands in remembrance and respect of one of the finest players ever to have put on the red shirt of Wales or play for London Welsh.

## International Caps

13 January 1906. England (3) 3 vs Wales (13) 16. Athletic Ground, Richmond.

13 February 1906. Wales (6) 9 vs Scotland (0) 3. National Stadium, Cardiff.

10 March 1906. Ireland (8) 11 vs Wales (3) 6. Balmoral Showgrounds, Belfast.

12 January 1907. Wales (13) 22 vs England (0) 0. St Helen's, Swansea.

2 February 1907. Scotland (0) 6 vs Wales (3) 3. Inverleith.

1 January 1910. Wales (21) 49 vs France (14 ) 14 St Helen's, Swansea.

**Second Lieutenant Fred Leonard Perrett**
**17th Bn Royal Welsh Fusiliers**
**Died 1 December 1918**
**Aged 27**
**Prop**
**Five Caps**

*'A True Welsh Heart'*

Fred Leonard Perrett was born on 9 May 1891, the son of George and Emma Perrett of Briton Ferry, South Wales. Perrett originally played rugby for his local club, Briton Ferry, before eventually playing joining Neath in September 1912. While a member of Neath he earned his first Welsh cap against the touring South Africa team. Wales ran the South Africans close but lost to a single penalty kick.

Perrett was reselected for Wales in the 1914 Five Nations' Championship, one of only two Welsh players to appear in all four matches of the campaign, the other being Neath teammate Glyn Stephens. The two complemented each other well, especially during line outs. The Welsh team lost the first game against England but won the final three games to finish second. Perrett may have been selected for further Wales matches, but turned professional at the end of the 1913/14 season, joining rugby league team Leeds (later moving to Hull) RLFC. He made his rugby league debut on 19 February 1913.

Perrett's league career was cut short by the outbreak of the First World War. He joined the newly-formed Welsh Guards and served in France from 19 February 1916. He was subsequently commissioned as a second lieutenant, and transferred to the 17th Battalion Royal Welsh Fusiliers with seniority from 27 June 1917. He was seriously injured and died of his wounds in a casualty clearing station a month after the Armistice. Perrett is often left out of lists of the Welsh international war dead due to his supposed defection to the professional game.

He is buried at Terlincthun British Cemetery, Wimille, France (XII. A.18).

His next of kin was given as his wife, Mrs H. G. Perrett, of 118, St George's Road, Hull.

## International Caps
14 December 1912. Wales (0) 0 vs South Africa (3) 3. National Stadium. Cardiff.
18 January 1913. Wales (0) 0 vs England (0) 12. National Stadium, Cardiff.
1 February 1913. Scotland (0) 0 vs Wales (3) 8. Inverleith.
27 February 1913. France (0) 8 vs Wales (3) 11. Parc des Princes.
8 March 1913. Wales (8) 16 vs Ireland (8) 13. St Helen's, Swansea.

**Sergeant Louis (Lou) Augustus Phillips
Royal Fusiliers
Died 14 March 1916
Aged 38
Scrum-half
Four Caps**

*'As true as steel'*

Louis Augustus Phillips was born on 24 February 1878 at Stow Hill, Newport, Monmouth and educated at Monmouth Grammar School after which he served his articles with Messrs Huberston and Fawckner, architects. Being elected ARIBA he started in practice in 1907. 'Lou' Phillips was one of the best-known internationals in Wales. He excelled at both water polo and cricket and started his rugby career playing for Monmouth Grammar School. Later his work as a half back, together with the legendary Llewellyn Lloyd, for Newport and Wales become the stuff of legend. He gained his place with the Newport XV in 1897/98, the same year in which J. J. Hodges and R.T. Skrimshire came to prominence. Between 1897/98 and 1900/01 he played for Newport RFC ninety times. Lou played scrum-half for Wales four times and made his international debut against England as part of Billy Bancroft's Triple Crown winning team in 1900. Unfortunately, while playing against Scotland in 1901, he damaged his knee badly which put an end to his International career.

Despite the disappointment, he wasn't the kind of man to sit down and remember past glories. An outstanding golfer, he won the Welsh amateur championship in both 1907 and 1912, was the runner-up in the Irish Championship in 1913 and was beaten in the sixth round of the Open Championship in 1914.

At the outbreak of war he enlisted into the ranks of the 20th Battalion Royal Fusiliers (3rd Public Schools Battalion). After training he was sent to France in November 1915 and, having refused a commission, became a sergeant (PS/5457). He was shot through the chest while out with a wiring party on the night of 14 March 1916. A friend said of him, 'nobody talked about his own athletic deeds less than he did … he was as true as steel, kind-hearted, loved by children and animals, and a sportsman in the best of terms'. There can be little doubt that he was one of the great scrum halves of all time.

He is buried in Cambrin Churchyard Extension, Pas de Calais, France (Grave L1.10B).

Thomas was engaged in the Mercantile Service, Calcutta, for three years, which he voluntarily gave up to join the forces in 1916. He was commissioned as a second lieutenant in the King's Royal Rifle Corps. However, like so many young officers, he didn't survive long, being killed in action at the battle of Guillemont on 3 September 1916. The sense of loss his family and friends felt is probably reflected through the letters he sent. The provost of King's College wrote:

> His whole career was one to be proud of ... I remember when we first saw him at King's, after he was tried for his choral scholarship, we all said we must have him in college. It was not only his voice; it was his bearing of gay modesty that won upon us; and ever since he kept his place in our hearts.

Thomas seemed to have a sense of his own mortality. In two letters he wrote to friends shortly before being killed, he said, 'I am not afraid of death at all, I feel a clean conscience. My life has been a truly happy one, thanks to you all from the bottom of my heart.'

Thomas's sister Rosalind served as a nurse, his brother John died of wounds, and his other brother, Morgan, won the MC.

His body was never recovered and his name is commemorated on the Thiepval Memorial (Pier and Faces 16B and 16C).

## International Caps

14 December 1912. Wales (0) 0 vs South Africa (3) 3. National Stadium, Cardiff.

18 January 1913. Wales (0) 0 vs England (0) 12. National Stadium, Cardiff.

**Second Lieutenant Philip (Phil) Dudley Waller**
**South African Heavy Artillery**
**71 Siege Battery**
**Died 14 December 1917**
**Aged 28 Wales**
**Forward**
**Six Caps**

*'Recognized by the distinction of a commission in the field'*

Philip Dudley Waller was born on 28 January 1889 at the Limes, Odd Down, Bath, the son of Mr A. P. and Mrs E. Waller, of 4 Glebe Terrace, Alloa, Scotland. He attended Carmarthen Intermediate School where he came to notice as a keen athlete. On leaving school in 1906 he was apprenticed as an engineer to the Alexander Dock Railway Company. While there he came to the notice of Thomas Pearson, a well-known international of the 1890s, who introduced him to Newport Rugby Football Club. Waller quickly became identified with Welsh rugby by becoming a regular member of the Newport XV. In 1907 he also played for Somerset County under his birth qualification. He was a clever forward in the loose and line-out although neither the scrum nor defensive play suited his style. He played for Wales in every match of the 1909 season and was part of the Welsh Triple Crown-winning side. He turned out again in 1910 to play against Australia and France. Later the same year he went to South Africa with a British Isles team, playing in twenty-three of the twenty-four matches. Waller must have enjoyed the country and experience because he decided to settle down in Johannesburg, working as an engineer under the Johannesburg municipality. Although not keen on the South African style he still became an active member of the Johannesburg Wanderers Football Club and captained their first XV for three seasons.

Waller joined up in March 1915 at Cape Town becoming a gunner in the South African Heavy Artillery, commanded by an old rugby antagonist, Major H. C. Harrison, the English international. On arriving in England he was stationed in Bexhill-on-Sea, going to the front in February 1916. In May 1917 he received a field commission for distinguished conduct. Waller was killed by a shell which also killed his major at Arras on 14 December 1917. His late commanding officer, Major Rann, later wrote to his father:

I knew him from the time of his enlistment in Cape Town, and was certain, after a time, his ability and personality would soon work for his promotion. As his Battery Commander I was glad when he could be recognized by the distinction of a commission in the field, and not only that, but be allowed to remain with his old Battery.

He is buried in Red Cross Corner Cemetery, Beugny, Pas de Calais, France (Grave I, F. 14).

## International Caps

12 December 1908. Wales (3) 9 vs Australia (3) 6. National Stadium, Cardiff.

16 January 1909. Wales (8) 8 vs England (0) 0. National Stadium. Cardiff.

6 February 1909. Scotland (0) 3 vs Wales (0) 5. Inverleith.

23 February 1909. France (0) 5 vs Wales (9) 47. Stade Olympique, Paris.

13 March 1909. Wales (0) 18 vs Ireland (0) 5. St Helen's, Swansea.

1 January 1910. Wales (21) 49 vs France (14) 14. St Helen's, Swansea.

6 August 1910. South Africa (3) 14 vs Great Britain (3) 10. Wanderers Ground, Johannesburg.

27 August 1910. South Africa (3) 3 vs Great Britain (0) 8. Crusaders Ground, Port Elizabeth.

3 September 1910. South Africa (5) 21 vs Great Britain (0) 5. Newlands Stadium, Cape Town.

**Corporal David Watts**
**7th Bn King's Shropshire Light Infantry**
**Died 14 July 1916**
**Aged 30**
**Lock**
**Four Caps**

*'In the heart of everything the men in red did'*

David Watts was born on 14 March 1886 in Maesteg, Bridgend, Wales into a coalmining family and lived with his grandparents, Samuel and Phoebe Jones, in Talbot Terrace, Maesteg (later moving to Garn Road in Maesteg). After leaving school he did what most boys of the town did and went down the pit. The 1901 census gives his profession as a coal hewer (aged sixteen ). Although it was a profession that had many problems, it also made men fit and very tough, the perfect ingredients for a top-class rugby player.

His local club, Maesteg Rugby Club, established in 1882 (although some records state 1877), was a short walk from his home and it was there that he began his career. He came to prominence as part of the Maesteg team that won the Glamorgan Challenge Cup in 1912, playing lock. Largely as a result of this, Watts was selected to represent Wales as part of the Five Nations' Championship in 1914. His first game was on 17 January against England at Twickenham. Wales introduced five new caps including David Watts. Wales's entire team only numbered fifty-six caps. England were also experimenting and gave debuts to six players but were more experienced with eighty caps in all and had in their team the supreme trio, Poulton-Palmer, Cyril Lowe and Charles 'Cherry' Pillman.

Wales played their next game on 7 February at Cardiff Arms Park against Scotland. Scotland were thoroughly beaten, but not without complaint. The Scottish captain, David Bain, received six stitches to a head wound and claimed 'The dirtier side won!' The Reverend Davies continued as captain of the ferocious 'Terrible Eight' and when asked whether he was ever offended by the 'colourful language' of the other seven he replied, 'I always wear a scrum cap!'

Wales went on to defeat France and then Ireland. Watts was described to have been 'in the heart of everything the men in red did'. This was the first ever time a pack had remained unchanged through a home championship. However, the 'Terrible Eight' would never play together again.

At the outbreak of the war, and despite being in a reserved occupation, Watts enlisted in Maesteg joining the 7th Bn King's Shropshire Light Infantry. Many of his rugby friends had enlisted, including the Reverend Alban Davies, who was an army chaplain with the Royal Artillery. The battalion landed in Boulogne on 15 October 1915 and Watts must have seen a lot of heavy fighting. The Shropshires were in reserve on 1 July 1916, the first day of the Somme offensive. However, two weeks later, they moved up the line to take part in the offensive to capture Bazentin Ridge. The official war history of the regiment recorded the following:

The night assembly and deployment of the assaulting battalions went without a hitch and by 11pm on the 13th of July the battalion was in position in no man's land waiting for dawn. The objectives were the enemy front trench and support line running through Bazentin le Grand, a distance of 1,500 yards. Owing to the undulation of the ground the enemy trenches were not visible. At 03:20 there was a brief preliminary bombardment, lasting 5 minutes, which was very short, and caused a number of casualties amongst our own men. Unfortunately, the attack ran into exceptionally strong, and quite uncut, wire about 600 yards from the front enemy trench. Not one man of the first wave succeeded in getting through this wire, of which there were two rows, each ten to twenty yards deep. The succeeding waves of attack closed on the first and the enemy had an easy target. After vain attempts to penetrate the wire, the remnants of the attacking force fell back to the shelter of the sunken road about 200 yards from the enemy trenches. About 11am the remnants of the battalion attacked again and, assisted by bombing parties from the flanks, succeeded in cutting their way through the wire, reaching the enemy trenches.

Sixteen officers were either killed or wounded, 147 other ranks were killed outright, 278 others were wounded (sixteen of whom subsequently died) and sixteen men were missing.

Like so many others, Davis Watts's body was never recovered and his name is recorded on the Thiepval Memorial France (Pier and Face 12 A and 12D). His name also appears on the Memorial Stone at the Millennium Stadium in Cardiff and, most proudly, at Llynfi Road, Maesteg, where his photograph resides above the bar in the members' lounge.

## International Caps
17 January 1914. England (5) 10 vs Wales (4) 9. Twickenham.

7 February 1914. Wales (7) 24 vs Scotland (5) 5. National Stadium, Cardiff.

2 March 1914. Wales (13) 31 vs France (0) 0. St Helen's, Swansea.

14 March 1914. Ireland (3) 3 vs Wales (3) 11. Balmoral Showgrounds, Belfast.

**Private David (Dai) Westacott**
**2/6th Bn The Gloucestershire Regiment**
**Died 28 August 1917**
**Aged 35**
**Forward**
**One Cap**

*'He certainly died as he lived, a true sportsman'*

David Westacott was born on 1 July 1882 in Cardiff. He first came to note as a rugby player when he was selected for his school side, Grangetown National, where he shone as a forward. In 1903 Westacott joined Cardiff and played for them for seven seasons, turning out no less than 120 times. In 1905 he was selected to play for his county side, Glamorgan, and formed part of the side to face the first touring New Zealand team. Wales had just beaten New Zealand in a match dubbed the 'Game of the Century' by the British press. Several of the Welsh internationals who had faced the All Blacks, reneged on a promise to turn out for the Glamorgan team and several positions needed to be filled quickly. Westacott was one of five Cardiff players to join the Glamorgan squad, none of whom had been part of the victorious Welsh team of five days earlier. Despite some early pressure from Glamorgan, and excellent work from Gibbs as an extra back, New Zealand won nine-nil. Even though he turned out for Glamorgan on 21 December, Westacott was not selected as a member of the Cardiff side to face the tourists just five days later.

After playing thirty games of the 1904/05 season for Cardiff, and facing the All Blacks for Glamorgan, Westacott was selected for his one and only international cap for the Wales team in the 1906 Home Nations' Championship. Wales had won the Triple Crown the previous season, and had already defeated both England and Scotland in the 1906 campaign; a win over Ireland would give the team back-to-back championships. The Welsh selectors changed the team formation by dropping Billy Trew from centre and bringing in an extra forward. Three new Welsh caps were brought into the pack, Westacott, Cardiff teammate Jack Powell and Llaneli's Tom Evans. The Irish played an incredible game and, even though they finished the game with only thirteen men on the field due to injuries, were still able to beat Wales by a five-point margin. Westacott was dropped for the next Wales international and never represented his country again.

Despite the fact that Westacott was no longer part of the Wales team, he continued playing for Cardiff and, in 1908, was part of the senior XV to face the 1908 touring Australian team. The game ended in the Australians' biggest loss of the tour, with Cardiff winning twenty four – nil. Westacott was at the centre of an on-pitch incident after Australian lock Albert Burge was sent off after 'brutally' kicking Westacott who was prone on the ground. Westacott continued to play for Cardiff until the 1909/10 season.

Westacott joined the Gloucestershire Regiment on 15 November 1914 and after training at Woolwich was sent to France in February 1915. He returned home a year later for a short period of leave. On 23 August 1916 he came home again, this time wounded, spending ten days at home before being stationed at Maidstone and Sittingbourne for a further eight months before returning to France. Westacott's company was part of a British advance on German positions at Springfield Farm on 27 August 1917 and came to notice for taking the bunker positions around the farm where they suffered heavy casualties. Westacott was killed in action the following day, His widow received the following letter from his Company Commander C. M. Hughes, regarding his death:

I much regret to inform you of the death in action of your husband, Private Westacott, of my company. He was killed by a shell in the support trenches on the 28th of last month. Death was instantaneous. He was buried in the proper manner the following day. I am very sorry indeed to lose him. He was a fine man, and one of the mainstays of the platoon. I had heard of his athletic fame, and he certainly died as he lived, a true sportsman. Please accept my most sincere sympathy.

Like so many men during the war his body was lost and he is commemorated on the Tyne Cot Memorial, Zonnebeke, West Vlaanderen, Belgium (Panels 72 to 75).

## International Caps
10 March 1906. Ireland (8) 11 vs Wales (3) 6. Balmoral Showgrounds, Belfast.

**Captain John Lewis Williams**
**16th Bn The Welsh Regiment**
**Died 12 July 1916**
**Aged 34**
**Captain/Wing**
**Seventeen Caps**

*'Be long remembered and mourned'*

John Lewis Williams was born on 3 January 1882 at Llwyncelyn Whitchurch, near Cardiff, the son of Edward Williams. He was educated at Cowbridge Grammar School, but his first games of rugby were for Whitchurch, where he played left wing three-quarter, a position he maintained throughout his career. John went on to play for Newport and played for both their second and first XV. In 1903/04 he joined the Cardiff Club and, in his first season, partnered with R. T. Gabe and scored ten tries and dropped one goal. During the 1904/5 and 1905/06 seasons he was Cardiff's leading try scorer while in the 1908/09 season he captained Cardiff. He also played for London Welsh, Harlequins and Glamorgan.

After leaving school he became one of the principals in the firm of Messrs Greenslade and Williams, coal exporters, based at Cardiff Docks. He went on to play for Wales seventeen times between 1906 and 1911, in which year he retired. A member of the British team that toured New Zealand and Australia in 1908 he wrote to the *South Wales Daily News* and *South Wales Echo* a series of articles describing incidents on that tour. Williams was noted for his side step and his inward swerve when running the touchline was a signature move. When the 1906 touring South Africans played Cardiff, he managed to side step the great Arthur Marsberg to score a try. As Williams walked back Marsberg was so impressed he approached him and shook his hand.

Williams was first capped in 1906 against the first-ever touring South African side. Although seen as one of the worst Welsh performances, the selectors kept faith in Williams and he would play for Wales a further sixteen times taking part in three Welsh Triple Crown winning sides, losing only two matches and scoring seventeen tries in his seventeen games. In the 1911 game against France, Billy Trew gave the captaincy to Williams (mainly because he could speak French). It was his greatest honour.

On 24 September 1914, shortly after the outbreak of the First World War, Williams joined the Public School Battalion of the Royal Fusiliers and began his training at Ashtead, Surrey. He received a commission as a second lieutenant in the 16th Battalion The Welsh Regiment (Cardiff City) in December 1914 and was sent to Colwyn Bay for training. He was promoted to lieutenant in February 1915 and captain the following March. He eventually proceeded to France on 1 December 1915. He became captain of C Company and was wounded in the leg while leading his men in an attack at Mametz Wood on 7 July 1916. On 12 July, just five days later, Williams died from his wounds at a casualty clearing station.

Williams is buried in Corbie Communal Cemetery Extension, Somme, France (Plot 1, Row C, Grave 31).

## International Caps

1 December 1906. Wales (0) 0 vs South Africa (6) 11. St Helen's, Swansea.

12 January 1907. Wales (13) 22 vs England (0) 0. St Helen's, Swansea.

2 February 1907. Scotland (0) vs Wales (3) 3. Inverleith.

9 March 1907. Wales (6) 29 vs Ireland (0) 0. National Stadium, Cardiff.

18 January 1908. England (8) 18 vs Wales (15) 28. Ashton Gate, Bristol.

1 February 1908. Wales (3) 6 vs Scotland (5) 5. St Helen's, Swansea.

14 March 1908. Ireland (5) 5 vs Wales (5) 11. Balmoral Showgrounds Belfast.

12 December 1908. Wales (3) 9 vs Australia (3) 6. National Stadium, Cardiff.

16 January 1909. Wales (8) 8 vs England (0) 0. National Stadium, Cardiff.

6 February 1909. Scotland (0) 3 vs Wales (0) 5. Inverleith.

23 February 1909. France (0) 5 vs Wales (9) 47. Stade Olympique, Paris.

13 March 1909. Wales (0) 18 vs Ireland (0) 5. St Helen's, Swansea.

12 March 1910. Ireland (3) 3 vs Wales (3) 19. Lansdowne Road, Dublin.

21 January 1911. Wales (5) 15 vs England (3) 11. St Helen's, Swansea.

4 February 1911. Scotland (4) 10 vs Wales (7) 32. Inverleith.

28 February 1911. France (0) vs Wales (0) 15. Parc des Princes.

11 March 1911. Wales (5) 16 vs Ireland (0) 0. National Stadium, Cardiff.

6 June 1908. New Zealand (21) 32 vs Anglo-Welsh (0) 5. Carisbrook, Dunedin.

27 June 1908. New Zealand (0) 3 vs Anglo-Welsh (0) 3. Athletic Park, Wellington.

# Bibliography and Sources

Bath, Richard, *The Scotland Rugby Miscellany* (Vision Sports Publishing Ltd, 2007)

Clutterbuck, L. A., *The Bond of Sacrifice, Vols 1 & 2* (Naval & Military Press, 2002)

Cooper, Stephen, *The Final Whistle: The Great War in Fifteen Players* (The History Press, 2013)

Creagh and Humphris, *The Victoria Cross 1856-1920* (Naval & Military Press, 2001)

Creagh and Humphris, *The DSO 1886-1923* (Naval & Military Press, 2001)

Dine, Philip, *French Rugby Football: A Cultural History* (Berg Publishers, 2001)

Edmonds, Brig-Gen J. E. (ed), *Official History of the Great War: Military Operations* (Imperial War Museum, 1992)

Gliddon, Gerald, *When the Barrage Lifts: A Topographical History of the Battle of the Somme* (Sutton Publishing, 1994)

Goodwin, Terry, *The International Rugby Championship 1883-1983* (Collins, 1984)

Goodwin, Terry, *The Complete Who's Who of International Rugby* (Cassell, 1987)

Henshaw, Trevor, *The Sky Their Battlefield: Complete List of Allied Air Casualties from Enemy Action in WWI* (Grub Street, 1995)

Keegan, John, *The First World War* (Pimlico, 1999)

de Klerk, Andrew, *International Rugby Encyclopedia* (30 Degrees South Publishers, 2009)

Lawson, Eric, *The First Air Campaign: August 1914-November 1918* (De Capo Press, 2002)

Mason, Tony and Riedi, Eliza, *Sport and the Military: The British Armed Forces 1880-1960* (Cambridge University Press, 2010)

Morris, Frank, *The First 100: A History of the London Scottish Football Club* (The London Scottish Football Club, 1977)

Pound, Reginald, *The Lost Generation* (Constable, 1964)

de Ruvigny, the Marquis, *The Roll of Honour Vols 1-5* (Naval & Military Press, 2013)

Sewell, E. D. H., *Rugby Football Internationals Roll of Honour* (T.C. & E.C. Jack, 1919)

Steel, Nigel and Hart, Peter, *Jutland, 1916: Death in the Grey Wastes* (Phoenix, 2004)

Strachan, Hew, *The First World War: A New History* (Free Press, 2006)

Thomas, Clem, *The History of the British Lions* (Mainstream Publishing, 1997)

## Websites
http://cwgc.org: Commonwealth War Graves Commission.

http://espnscrum.com: includes an online rugby database

## School and other Memorial Books
Eton College.

Rugby College.

Winchester College.

Oxford University Roll of Honour.

Cambridge University Roll of Honour.

## Other
The British Library Newspaper Library.